Product Design Now: Renderings

Cristian Campos

Product Design Now: Renderings

Cristian Campos

COLLINS DESIGN
An Imprint of HarperCollins Publishers

Product Design Now: Renderings
Copyright © 2010 by Collins Design and **maomao** publications

First Edition:
Published by **maomao** publications in 2010
Via Laietana, 32, 4.°, of. 104
08003 Barcelona, Spain
Tel.: +34 932 688 088
Fax: +34 933 174 208
mao@maomaopublications.com
www.maomaopublications.com

English language edition first published
in 2010 by:
Collins Design
An Imprint of HarperCollins*Publishers*,
10 East 53rd Street
New York, NY 10022
Tel.: (212) 207-7000
Fax: (212) 207-7654
collinsdesign@harpercollins.com
www.harpercollins.com

Distributed throughout the world by:
HarperCollins*Publishers*
10 East 53rd Street
New York, NY 10022
Fax: (212) 207-7654

Publisher:
Paco Asensio

Editorial Coordination:
Anja Llorella Oriol

Editor & texts:
Cristian Campos

Translation:
Cillero & de Motta

Art Direction:
Emma Termes Parera

Layout:
Maira Purman

Cover design:
Maira Purman

Cover art:
ding3000

Backcover art:
Benjamin Hubert
Bas van Leeuwen, Mireille Meijs
AquiliAlberg
ding3000
Amy Hunting
BY:AMT
Yariv Sade, Arik Yuval/Igloo Design
Antonija Jurinec Campbell

Library of Congress Control Number: 2010923476
ISBN: 978-0-06-196876-1

Printed in Spain

First Printing, 2010

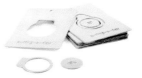

Introduction: How to Be a Design Genius

The childlike myth of innate creativity can be disregarded. Science has provided enough proof throughout recent decades that what we human beings call "artistic talent" is nothing more than the result of tens of thousands of years of evolutionary process and, obviously, a good deal of hard work. As Edward O. Wilson said with regard to Marxism: "Good theory. Wrong species."

Glancing over the designs included in this book, one could be tempted to attribute such creativity to "an innate stroke of genius." It is really a consolidating idea: if you have that mythical spark of genius within, then you don't have to make any effort at all as the results will flourish without having to lift a finger. And if out of bad luck you do not have that spark of genius, then we don't have to worry too much about lifting a finger as all the work will be in vain. What makes this myth so reassuring is that we either have the genius stroke or not; we don't need to worry about spending an extra second working or putting in extra effort. It is an appetizing idea for all types of soul savers: we cannot free ourselves from our destiny because we all fit into a predetermined mold.

Our objective when putting together this book was not to strip the illusion of youngsters allergic to work or fanatics of predetermination, but to simply show that good ideas and excellent designs are not made out of thin air. They are the result of a long process of trial and error of dozens of rejected sketches and a giant chain of ruled-out links. It is perhaps not a very romantic idea, but it is definitely more like the reality of our species.

Product Design Now: Renderings includes a wide range of designs and prototypes created by some of the best international designers in recent years. The book places importance on variety rather than homogeneity, which implies that the reader, when flipping through the pages, can come across an apparently simple design and then, in the next few pages, a complex unit. Some designers work with sketches previously hand-drawn, others with renderings (digital prototypes) and others with both. The majority of products in this book have been produced and are on sale, but a few of them are only prototypes or limited editions made to order.

If after reading this book, you still think that creativity is innate and does not depend on the hard work that goes with it, then we would like to remind you that what does seem to be completely innate is...the resistance to accept reality.

—Cristian Campos

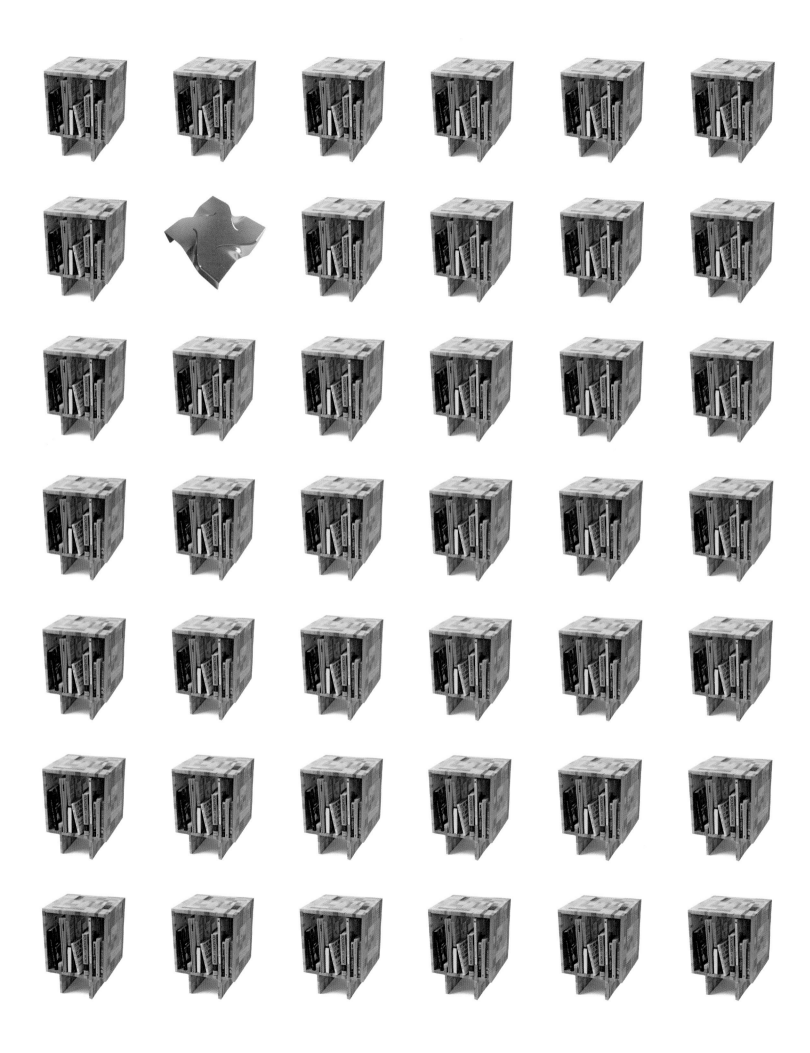

Furnishings and Fixtures

Animal Tales

ding3000 (2008)
*www.ding3000.com
info@ding3000.com*

ding3000 believe that Mother Nature is the best designer on the planet. The Animal Tales furniture collection is inspired by the "best creations" of the animal world. The Tazi sofa, for example, references the hair of an Afghan bloodhound; the Cuckoo vase imitates the gaping beak of a chick; the Giraffe lamp is inspired by the animal of the same name; and the side table by a pack mule. The base of Giraffe lamp is made of lacquered steel tubes. The shade is made of a pvc-cotton-laminate. The results are both spectacular, playful, and, above all else, empathetic.

Sketches from the design process
of the Jirafa lamp after the general
concept of the lamp was found.

The Cuckoo Vase is available in two sizes and is made of white porcelain. The inside of the "beak" is a copper-colored lacquer.

Sketches of the various developmental stages of the Cuckoo vase, including a whimsical drawing of a creature "feeding" the vase. ding3000 is interested in how people will have fun and interact with their products.

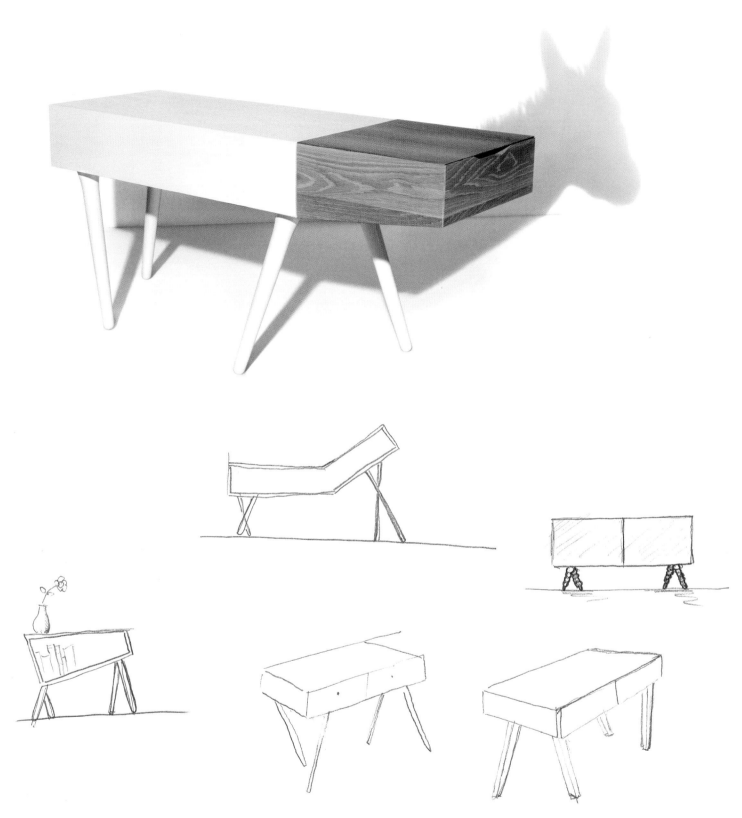

The Muli table is made from oak wood and has a large drawer and a compartment closed by a lid that can be accessed from the top of the table. The angles of the table's legs give the sensation that the Muli could walk away at any second.

First rough sketch of the construction of the Tazi sofa after the general design was determined.

Billy Wilder

ding3000 (2005)
www.ding3000.com
info@ding3000.com

As a tribute to Ikea's Billy shelf, which has sold more than forty-two million units worldwide, ding3000 launched the Billy Wilder. Inspired by the sharp twists and turns of tree branches, the Billy Wilder is jauntily chaotic—the perfect storage spot for unconventional books and magazines. In a sense, the shelf is a humoristic approach to the phrase "our daily mess."

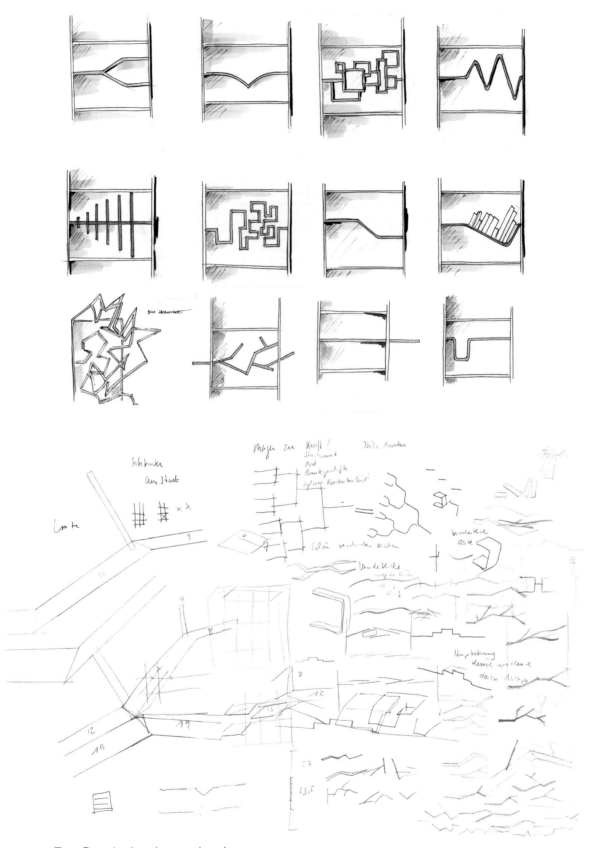

Top: Rough sketches and early conception ideas for the Billy Wilder shelf. Bottom: After settling on the design direction of a branch, ding3000 explored different linear configurations.

The sketches on this page clearly show the starting point and the formal reference on which the Billy Wilder shelf has been based: the twisted and chaotic branches of a tree.

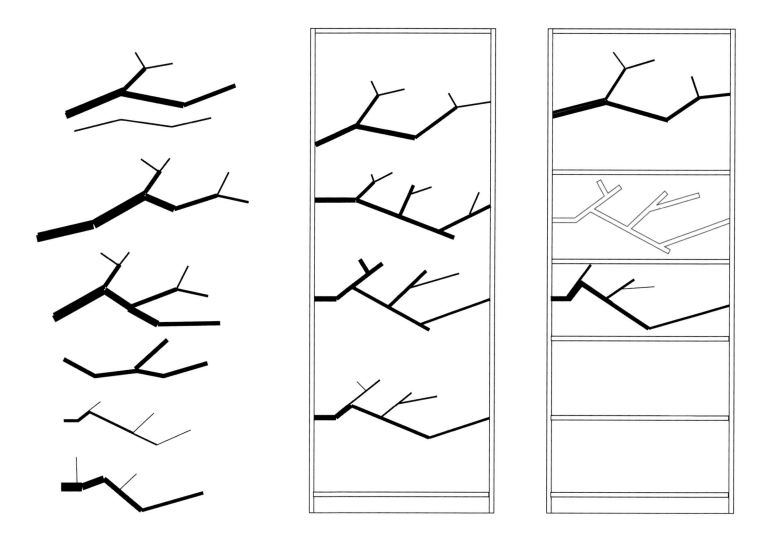

Sketches are transformed into 2-D, showing the shelf's real proportions and design application.

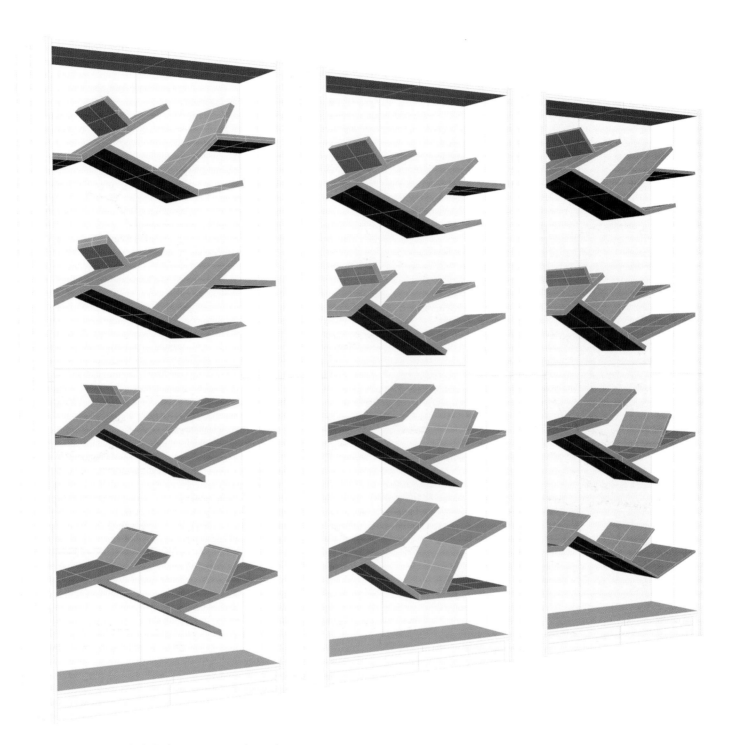

2-D drawings and sketches are transferred into 3-D. The designers are then able to judge the proportions and overall shape before making a physical model.

Capra

Michael Young (2007)

www.michael-young.com
contact@michael-young.com

For some time, the Accupunto brand has toyed with the idea of designing and producing a commercially viable, contemporary bar stool. After several years of researching ergonomics and testing the best combi-nation of wood and plastic materials, designer Michael Young created the Capra bar stool. Young's research paid off: the materials seamlessly meld into each oth-er and the seat is perfectly rounded into shape.

Chrysalis

One & Co (2008)

www.oneandco.com
hello@oneandco.com

Designed for the San Francisco-based company Council, the Chrysalis stool is light yet robust. The unique geometry of its legs and footrest give it a distinct and iconic posture. The footrest is on an incline—and isn't horizontal as with many similar stools—so that the unusual stance of the legs is highlighted. The seat comes in both leather or fabric; the body is stainless steel. At once formal yet simple in design, the Chrysalis is a iconic addition to any living space.

Clock Delay

Bas van Leeuwen (2008)
www.bloomming.com
info@studiobloomm.com

Clock Delay is analogical, has a retro-futuristic look, and is electronic. Its mechanism has three different cogwheels: one marks the hour, the other, the minutes, and the third, the seconds. The intersection point of the three wheels displays the exact time.

Clock Delay has been manufactured in stainless steel and aluminum, and its objective is to be a visual feast for people interested in and lovers of technology. As stylish as it is innovative, Clock Delay is more than a clock; it is an objet d'art.

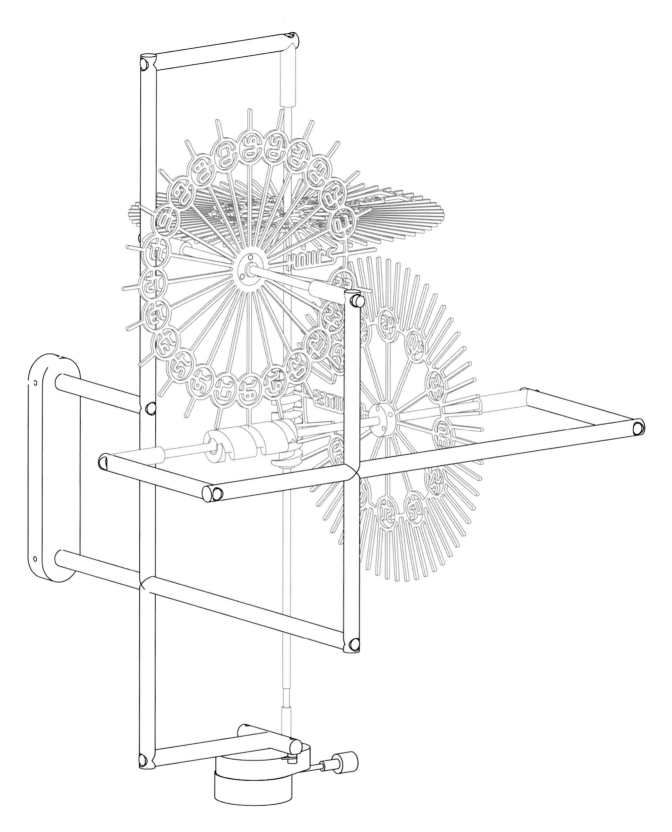

These detailed sketches illustrate the mechanism of the intersection of the three cogged wheels and the intricate representations of their numbers.

Clock Delay is made of stainless steel
and aluminum, and measures 13.8"
in length, 13.8" in width, and 18.9" in
height. To adjust the time, you can pull
and turn the hours wheel to the right
time.

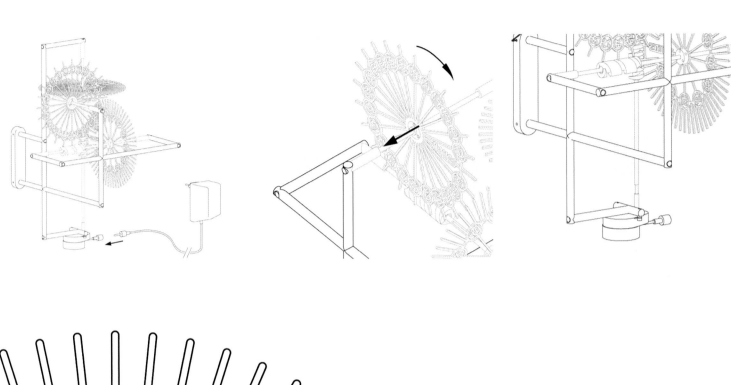

Every tooth of the Clock Delay
represents one minute. To adjust the
time, simply pull and wind the hours
wheel.

Cloud

Richard Hutten (2008)
www.richardhutten.com
info@richardhutten.com

Cloud represents part of the research Richard Hutten conducted on the idea of basic forms—in this case, the circle and the sphere. Hutten first created basic sketches of the chair. Two scale models—1:10 and 1:7—allowed the design team to work on finishing touches and final modifications. Manufactured in nickel-plated aluminum, Cloud has been designed to be extremely longwearing. Besides the two prototypes, only eight copies of this chair have been produced.

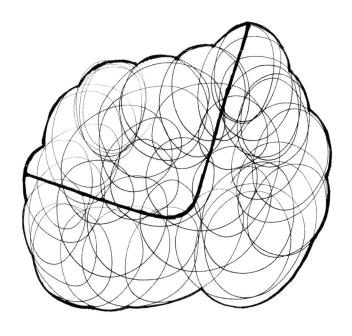

Cloud Chair   Richard Hutten

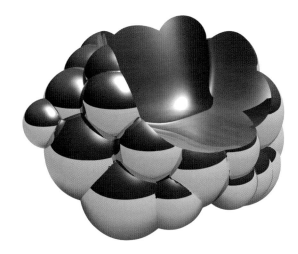

Crystal

Maria & Igor Solovyov (2008)

www.solovyovdesign.com
sigoryx@yahoo.com

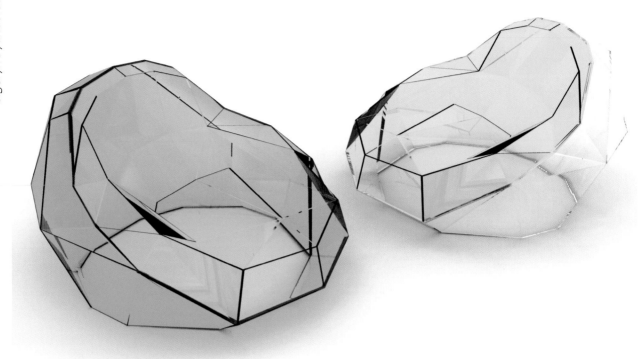

The Crystal seat has been manufactured with two independent plastic pieces; the first is a striking color and the second is totally transparent. The two components are welded together to give a visual sensation of unity without joints.

The combination of colors can be changed at the consumer's request. Designed to resemble the sharp edges of a crystal of a carved diamond, the chair is a stand-out piece in any interior space.

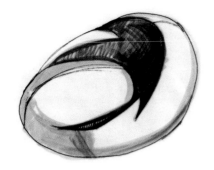

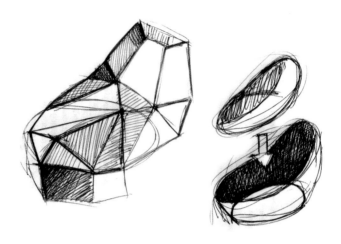

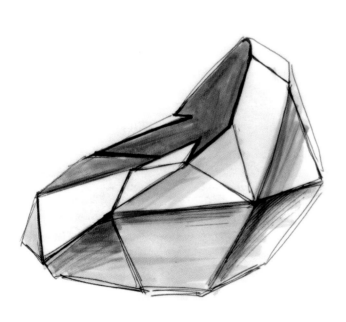

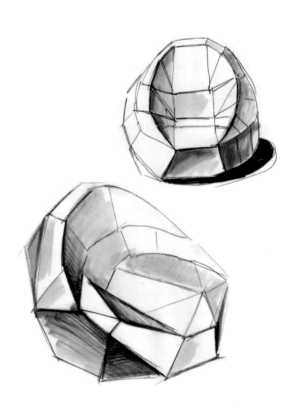

Diamond

Benjamin Hubert (2008)
www.benjaminhubert.co.uk
benjamin@benjaminhubert.co.uk

Diamond is an informal seat with metallic legs and a wood-finished back. The buttoned upholstery, available in five colors, gives the seat a retro style that contrasts strongly with the avant-garde aesthetics of the legs and the back. The crossed-leg system is similar to that used in other products designed by Benjamin Hubert. Like the Lily Pad table, it is available in two sizes and in different heights. Seen on the opposite page, the Lily Pad visually complements the simple aesthetic of the Diamond seat.

Endoskeleton

Alon Meron (2008)
www.alonmeron.com
alon@alonmeron.com

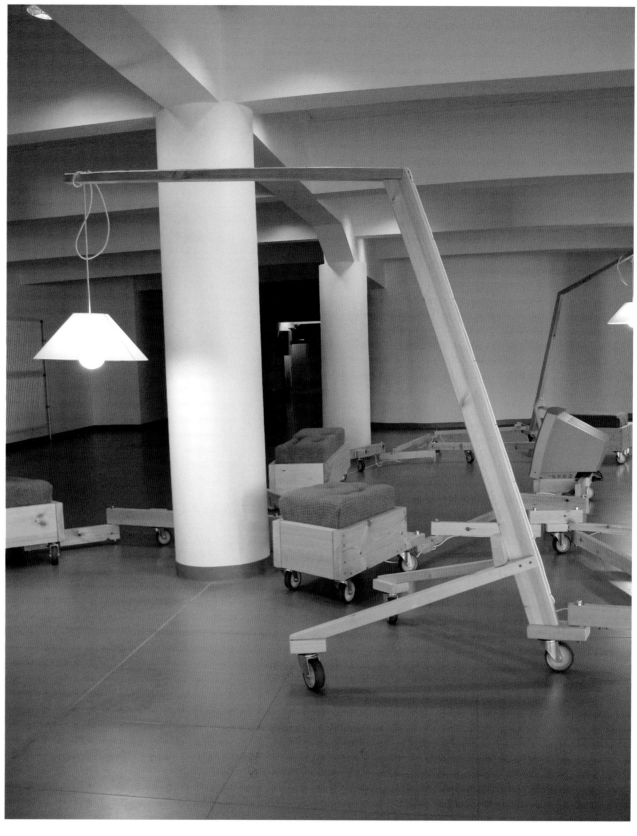

Endoskeleton is a living system that incorporates domestic elements into a mobile structure. This structure moves and creates particular spaces within and around itself. The concept of Endoskeleton is based on the idea that people follow determined and practically unchangeable routes inside their home. In this sense, it is a "personified" map of these routes: it suggests a determined way of moving about the space and fulfilling the functions of the objects that it contains (seats, television, lamps, etc.). The step from sketch to physical object occurred completely intuitively. The main concerns were those that concerned stability and ease of use.

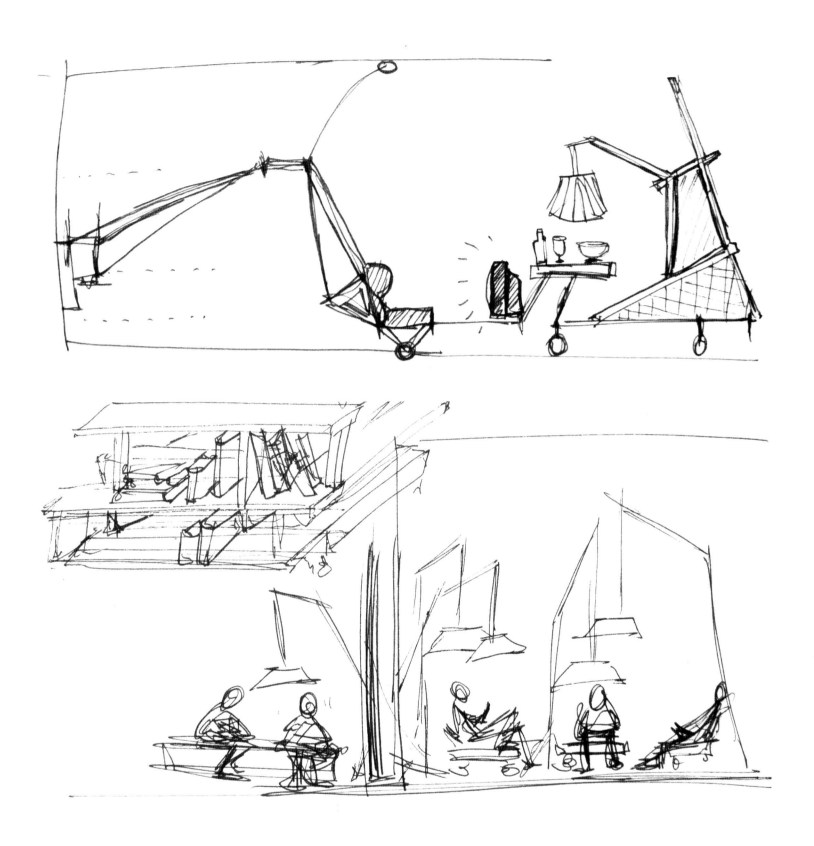

Sketches for Endoskeleton, a loose study
of different elements in the structure and
how it accommodates people. Very basic
materials were used: silent polyurethane
wheels, solid softwood, and coarse weave
wool fabric.

Iris

Charlie Davidson (2008)
www.charlie-davidson.com
mail@charlie-davidson.com

Designer Charlie Davidson came up with the idea of Iris when, one day, the sun's light rebounded off a fluorescent card sitting on his desk. Pink reflections danced on the wall. The effect was so powerful that Davidson was inspired to create an installation that similarly played with light, color, and luminous reflections. The first prototype of Iris was manufactured with cards and soldered micro wires. The tightened wires curve the base of the structure and reflect the light, casting an illuminating display of vibrant color and shadow.

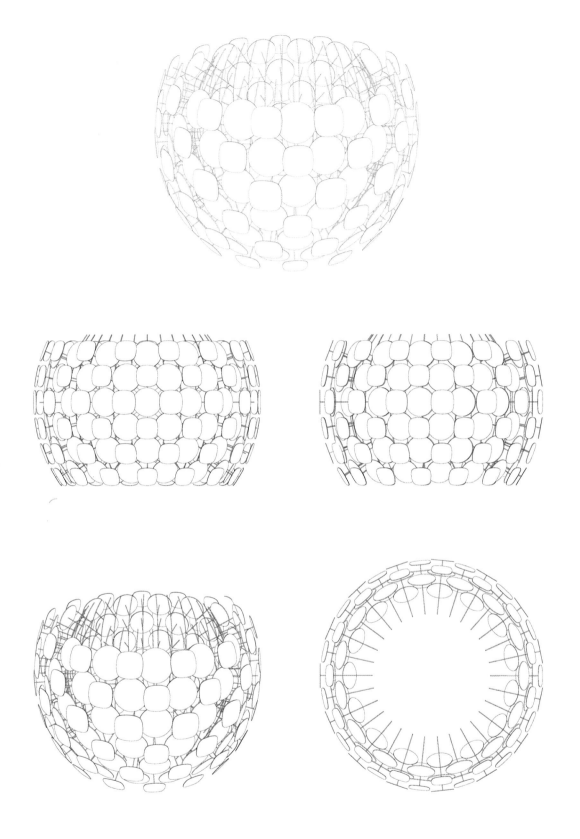

Fully detailed production drawings produced to work out the size, shape, and spacing of the 180 reflective surfaces or components of the Iris ceiling lamp.

Lightfacet

Mireille Meijs (2009)
www.bloomming.com
info@studiobloomm.com

Lightfacet is a modular system used to separate living spaces. Its individual elements are diamond-shaped and can rotate separately, playing with light and color in an endless array of combinations. While Lightfacet was originally designed as a curtain to divide spaces, it can also be used as a blind or as decoration. The structure can be as big (or as small) as the user wishes—more elements can be added to increase its size.

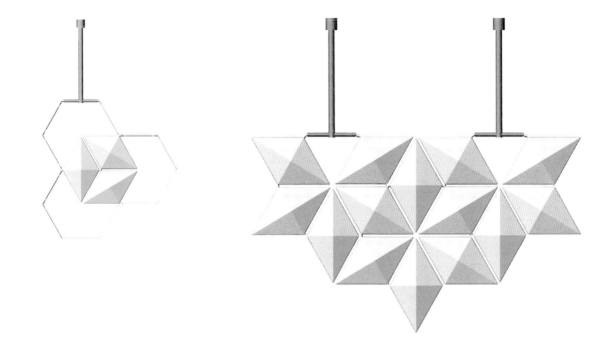

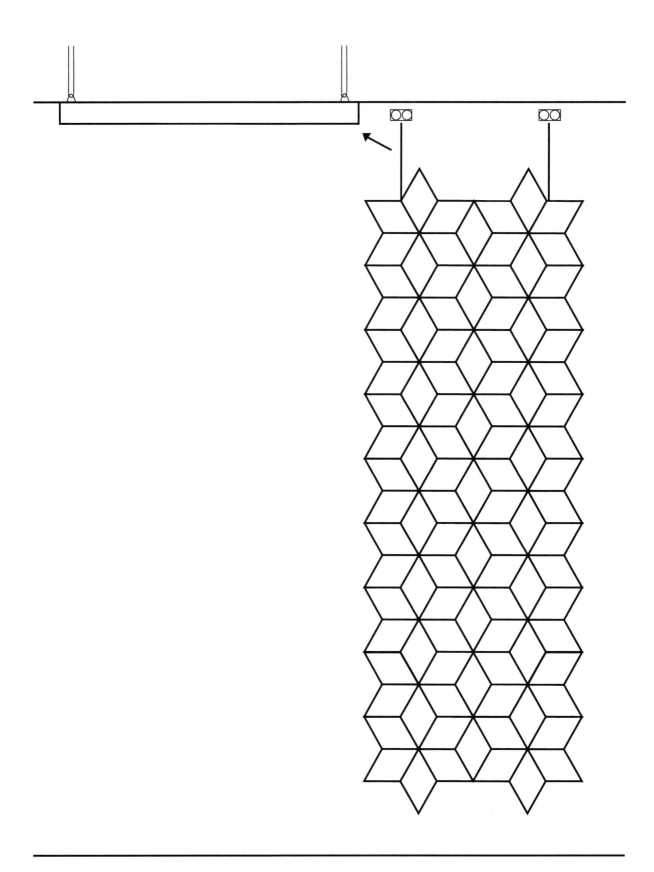

Lightfacet is hung from the ceiling by three
thin bars that are located at a fixed distance
from each other. While symmetrical in design,
Lighfacet also appears randomly constructed.

Loop

David Larsson (2008)
www.davidlarsson.com
david@davidlarsson.com

The Loop chair is a tribute to the veneered wooden chairs typical of the fifties. It appears to be made from just one piece, although it has actually been made from two, with the joining points concealed. The aim of the design was to solve the problem of the imperfection of the proportions, which had the effect of making the legs appear shorter than normal. After raising the front of the seat to give a sensation of lightness, the final design was settled upon: a balanced and comfortable chair with a definite personality.

First doodles of Loop. Once the overall design concept is determined, the design is further modified to account for the height and angle of the seat in relation to the backrest as well as the two "holes" in the front and back of the chair.

This sketch illustrates the assembly of the backrest to the main body of the chair. The backrest's wedge shape adds a "light feeling" to the final design.

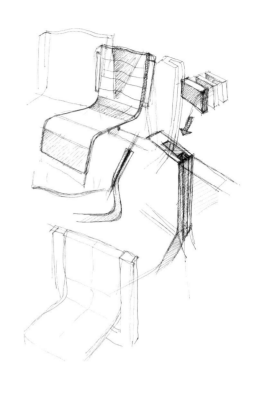

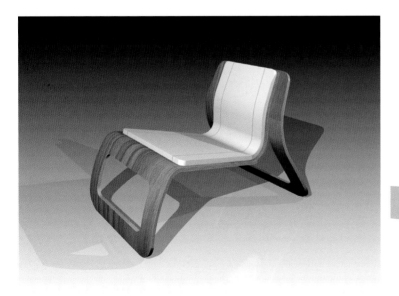

The 3-D rendering on the left shows the design coming together. The rendering on the right is an improved model, where the seat has been elevated and the backrest has been raised.

Manager's Chair

Ken Sugimoto, Adam Wade, Myk Lum/LDA (2007)

www.ldallc.com
mykl@ldallc.com

The Manager's Chair has been specifically designed for the "beginner's market," comprised of first-time product users. Consumer research has shown that design plays an important role in this market sector. To create the streamlined look of the Manager's Chair, the design team researched the work environments where this chair would most likely be located, taking into account various ergonomic factors and conditions.

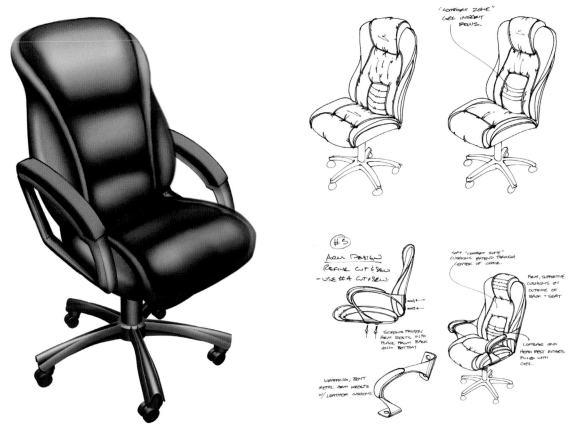

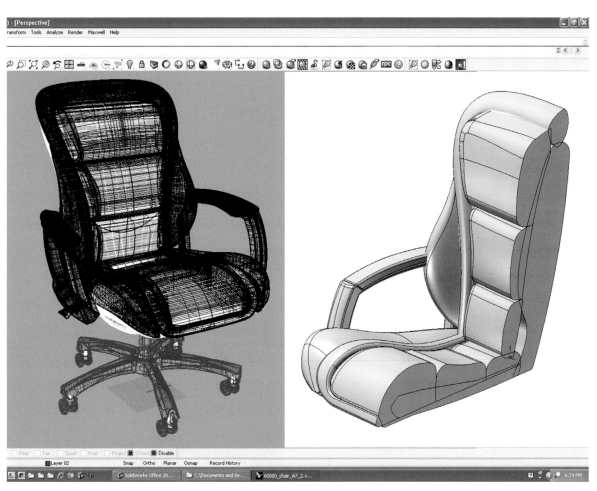

Packaging Lamp

David Gardener (2008)
www.davidgardener.co.uk
david@davidgardener.co.uk

The idea of the Packaging Lamp emerged when creator David Gardner discovered how many businesses overpackage their products. Packaging Lamp has been made with 100 percent recycled products. To ship, Packaging's main structure holds the cable, the low-consumption bulb, and the bulb holder. When the user opens the packaging and unpacks the components, he must slot them into their actual positions. The packaging of the lamp, then, becomes the lamp itself.

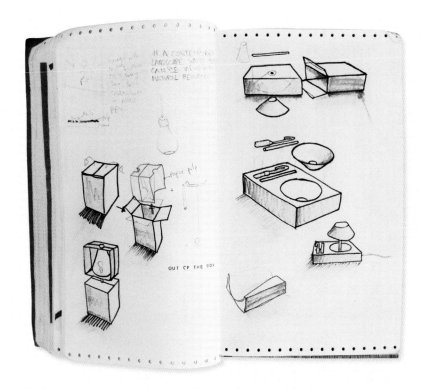

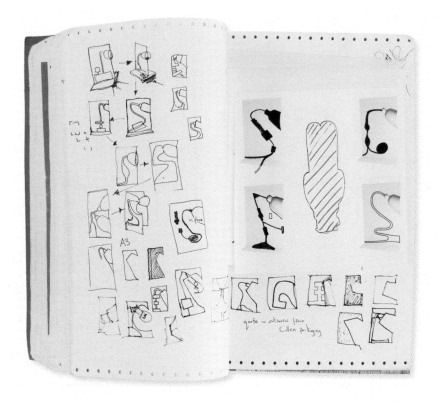

Preliminary sketches for the
Packaging Lamp drawn by designer
David Gardener in its design journal
that show the research done on all
the possible designs.

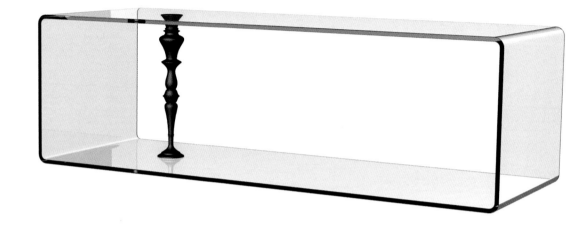

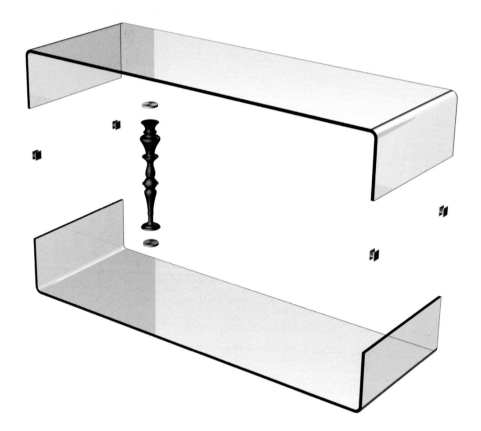

The Spindle table is a tribute to two opposing styles: minimalism and ornamentalism. The juxtaposition is not trying to be ironic or humoristic, but respectful to the history and the importance of both styles. Brad Ascalon Studio NYC considered dozens of possibilities and worked on a multitude of sketches, small models, and renderings before opting for the definitive model. The table has been made from glass 0.39 inches thick, lacquered wood, and steel. Measurements are 14.6 inches high, 49.2 inches long, and 16.9 inches wide.

Amy Hunting (2008)
www.amyhunting.com
hello@amyhunting.com

The Patchwork Collection

How can something valuable be created from industrial waste? Amy Hunting gathered wood from several Danish factories without having a clear idea of what she was going to do with it. A short while later, she began experimenting. The end result of her experimentation is The Patchwork Collection, a family of wooden furniture inspired by the idea of patchwork. Manufactured with fifteen different types of untreated wood to achieve the patchwork effect, the limited-edition collection has received alot of media attention for its innovative use of materials.

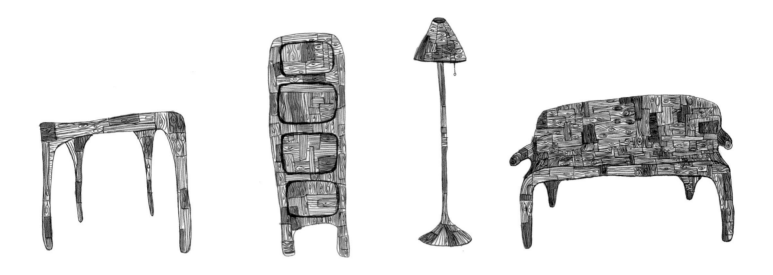

Vertigo

AquiliAlberg (2007)

www.aquilialberg.com
info@aquilialberg.com

Inspired by the work of Dutch artist M. C. Escher and his imaginary worlds, Vertigo appears otherworldly. Made from polyurethane, its shiny, lacquered finish make it unlike any other side table. Designed to provoke the visual illusion of continuously rotating surfaces, Vertigo is, in the words of its creators AquiliAlberg, "the sensation that the environment around you moves, when really nothing is moving. Vertigo suggests the illusion of movement." Measurements are 35.4 inches wide, 35.4 inches long, and 10.6 inches high.

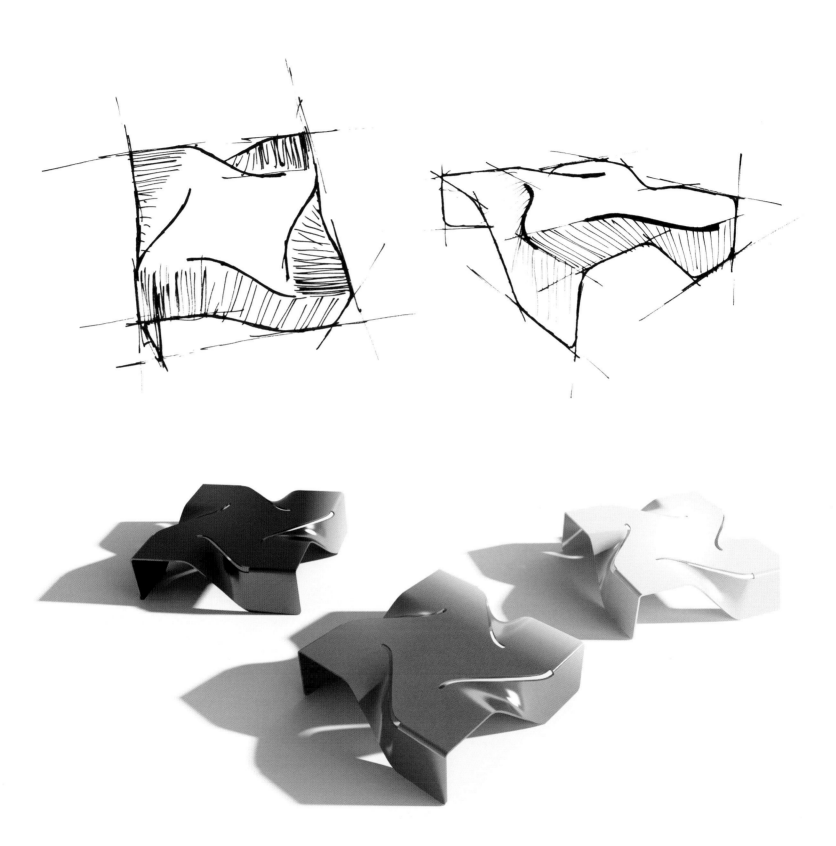

Vipp

Amy Hunting (2007)
www.amyhunting.com
hello@amyhunting.com

Vipp is a prototype of a rocking chair that allows the user to sit normally but also balance forwards and backwards. Made completely from wood, the chair is, from a design perspective, quite simple; it does not require the use of hooks or magnets to achieve the balancing effect. Designer Amy Hunting drew more than fifty sketches before arriving at the prototype seen here.

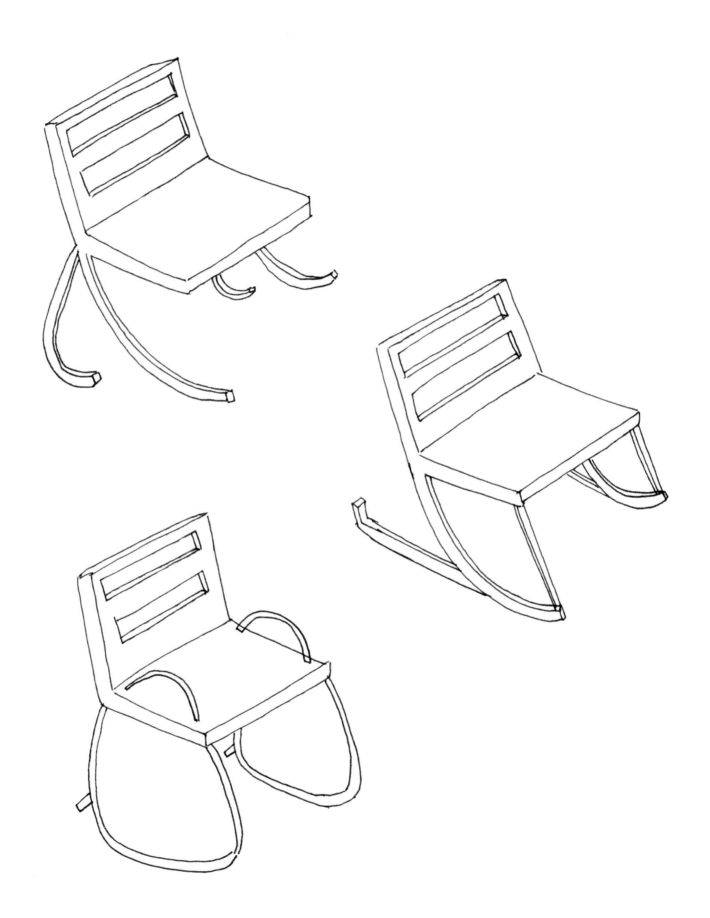

Zero Gee Lussedia

Gianni Orsini/WeLL Design (2007)

www.welldesign.com
info@welldesign.com

Zero Gee Lussedia is a luxury recliner that imitates the position of the body while relaxing in a weightless situation. It is equipped with an electric lumbar support. With this lumbar support the spine is always in the perfect position and it reduces stress on muscles and joints to a minimum. Lussedia is a fusion of Italian words: *lusso* meaning "luxury" and *sedia* meaning "seat." Zero Gee Lussedia is, in this sense, a tribute to the world of ostentation. Hand-made with the finest materials (German leather and silk, with 24-carat gold detailing), Zero Gee Lussedia stands out for its avant-garde ergonomics. Developed in collaboration with Delft University of Technology, the chair was unveiled at Amsterdam's Millionaire Fair in 2008.

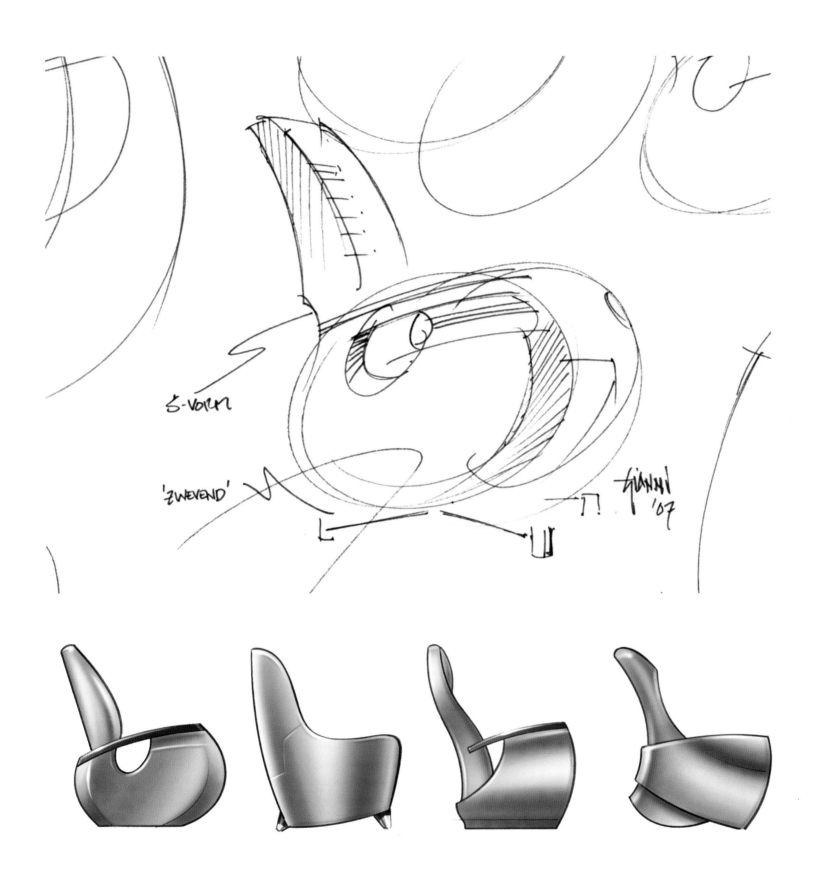

'S-VORM'

'ZWEVEND'

GIANNI '07

Four different design sketches for Zero Gee Lussedia. The sketch on the left is the final design. The chair doesn't rock, but does allow the user to recline.

Kitchen, Bathroom, and Office Appliances and Tools

ATE

Paul Sandip (2007)

www.coroflot.com/paulsandip, www.differentialdesign.blogspot.com
differentialdesign@yahoo.com

Using the phrase "Who ate my pencil?" as a conceptual jump-off point, ATE is Paul Sandip's playful take on the traditional pencil sharpener. ATE is, in short, what remains when the excess material of the pencil sharpener is removed; that is, two opposite cones, joined together at their narrowest end containing a blade. Two rubber hoops around the holes give the user a better grip and its satin finish gives it a personality and a quasi-futuristic appearance. ATE won a Red Dot prize in 2007.

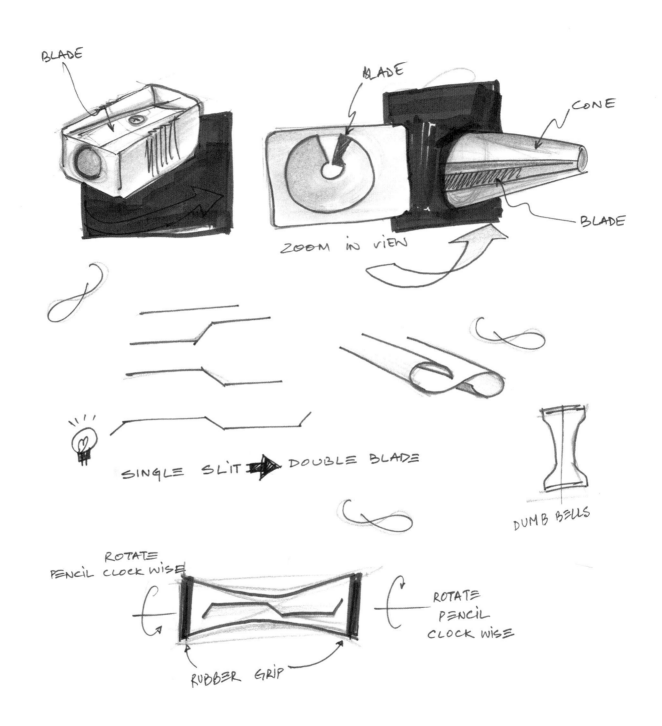

BLADE

BLADE

CONE

BLADE

ZOOM IN VIEW

SINGLE SLIT ▶ DOUBLE BLADE

DUMB BELLS

ROTATE
PENCIL CLOCK WISE

ROTATE
PENCIL
CLOCK WISE

RUBBER GRIP

Banat Toothbrushes

Kilit Tasi Design (2005)
www.kilittasi.com
info@kilittasi.com

Acrobat, Sweepy, and Tri-Action toothbrushes, designed by Kilit Tasi Design, feature a series of technological innovations that have revolutionized the normal standards of this type of product. The model seen here has two "handles" that secure the brush vertically to the edge of the glass, instead of inside it, helping the water to easily strain off and making the brush more hygienic. The curved shaped of the handle guarantees a perfect grip and prevents the user's hand from slipping.

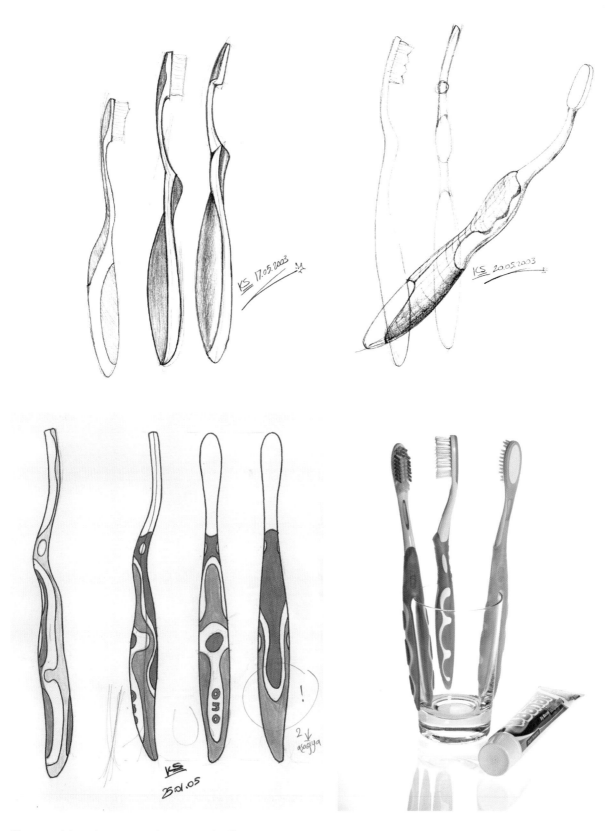

The toothbrushes seen here are inclined at different angles, allowing the bristles to reach parts of the mouth that could not be reached if they were parallel to the handle.

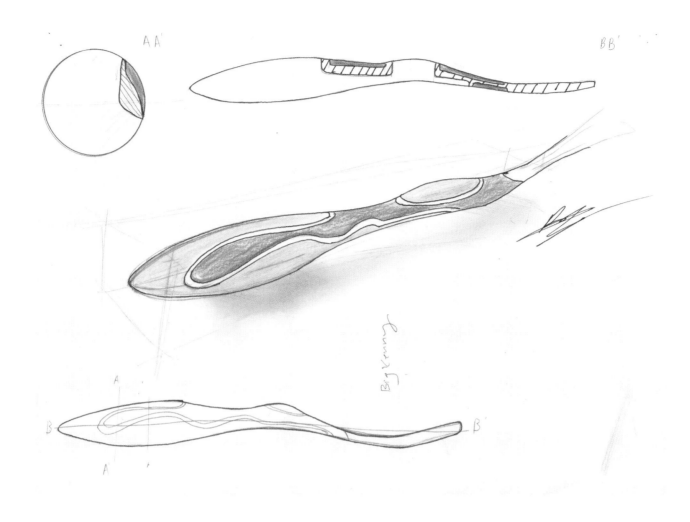

The flexible head structure was inspired by the two-boned system between our elbows and wrists. This quality provides extra flexibility to the head of the toothbrush around the body axis and minimizes the pressure of the bristles on the gums.

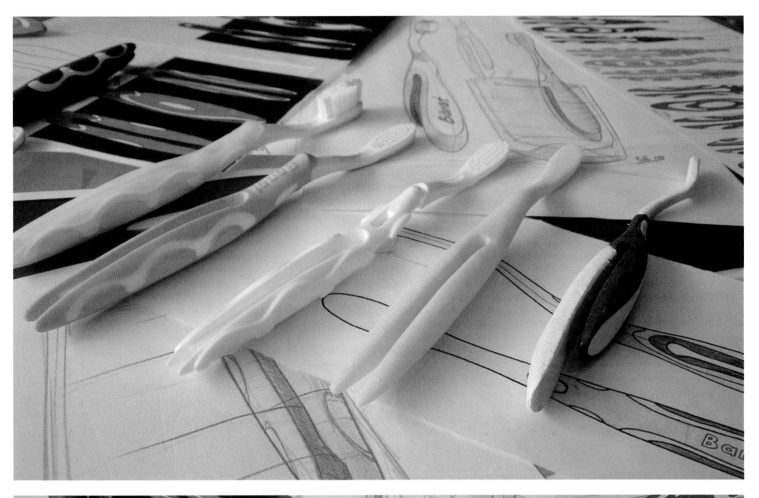

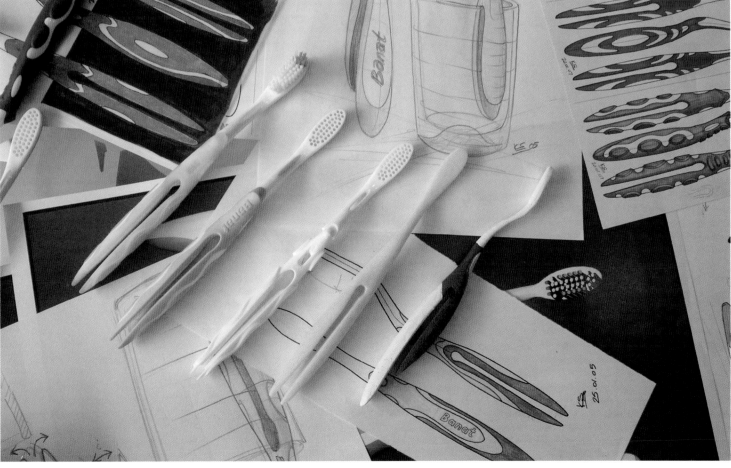

Bread Bin

Adrian and Jeremy Wright (2005)

www.designwright.co.uk
studio@designwright.co.uk

Bread Bin, made from glass and walnut wood, can be used as both a bread bin and a cutting board. The block of wood that is the base can be used as a surface to cut food when it is turned over. The contents of the bread bin are hidden by the grooved glass. The product's minimalist silhouette brings an element of sleek, avant-garde design to the modern kitchen table.

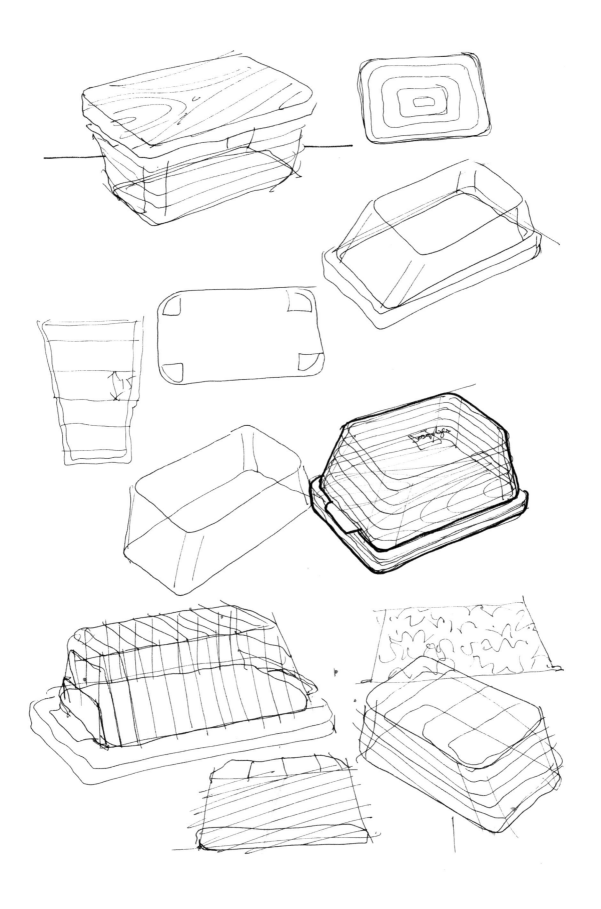

Clip

Paul Sandip (2007)

www.coroflot.com/paulsandip, www.differentialdesign.blogspot.com
differentialdesign@yahoo.com

Clip is the materialization of an idea by Paul Sandip, who wanted to create an object that was not only beautiful but also well-designed and functionable. Made with recycled plastic, Clip allows the user to hang up clothes from either one of its ends. That way, if, for any reason, one of the ends breaks, the other end can be used, thus prolonging the life of the device. Specifically designed with the Indian market in mind, yet applicable to markets all around the world, Clip is truly a forward-thinking product. In 2007, it won the San Francisco Organic Awards.

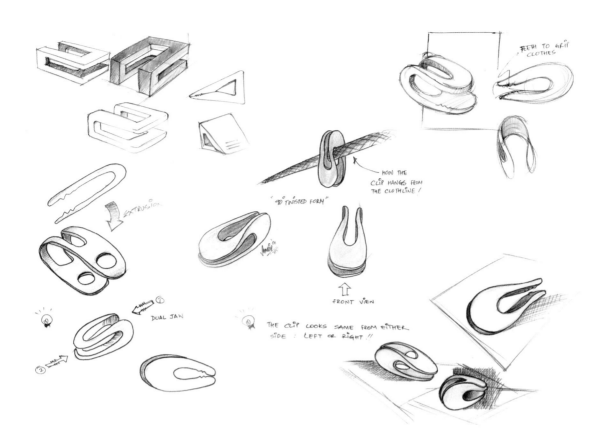

TEETH TO GRIP CLOTHES

EXTRUSION

"90° TWISTED FORM"

HOW THE CLIP HANGS FROM THE CLOTHLINE!

FRONT VIEW

DUAL JAW

THE CLIP LOOKS SAME FROM EITHER SIDE : LEFT OR RIGHT !!

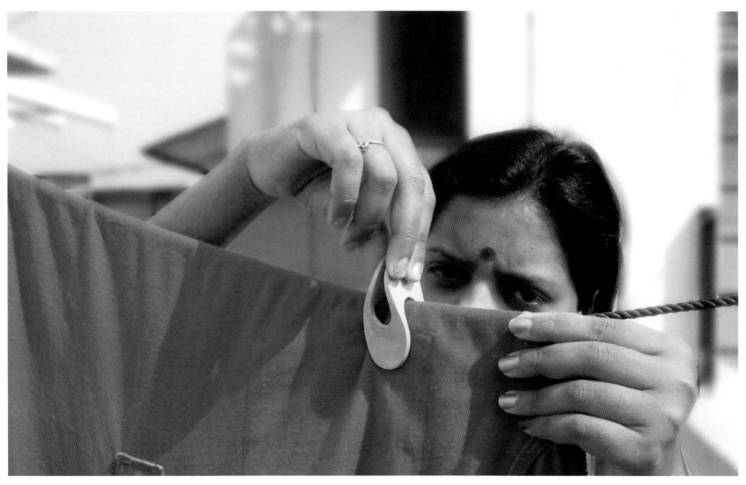

Curved Sushi

Kevin Kraemer (2006)
www.coroflot.com/kevinkraemer
kraemer.kevin@gmail.com

As its name indicates, Curved Sushi is a dish for sushi. Its design was requested by a Japanese restaurant that wanted one plate to hold the sushi, soy sauce, ginger, and wasabi. Curved Sushi has been manufactured by the process of slip casting, a low-cost, mass-production technique for ceramic items. This system can create three different plate sizes with a single mould, and, as they are reversible, organize different modular sets. The result is as simple as it is elegant.

SOY SAUCE

GINGER/WASABI

CHOPSTICK

Curved Sushi is reversible. The curve of the plate is designed to be very subtle so when it is reversed the sushi will not fall off. The bottom of the plate has a intergraded stand that elevates the plate slightly.

Dual

Adrian and Jeremy Wright (2007)

www.designwright.co.uk
studio@designwright.co.uk

Dual is a two-in-one chopping board made from molded polypropylene and beech wood, which allows the user to cut different types of food without mixing or contaminating flavors. The two boards are joined together by a patented magnetic system, which enables easy separation for flexible use and cleaning. Dual won the prestigious Design Plus award at the Ambiente show in Frankfurt in 2007.

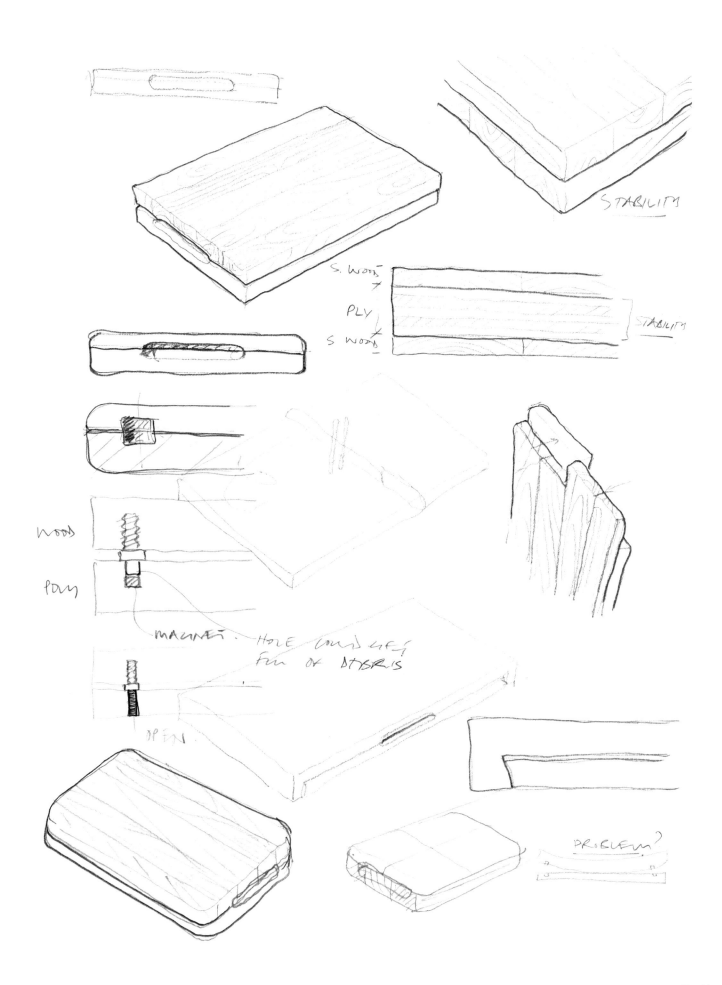

STABILITY

S. WOOD

PLY

S WOOD

STABILITY

WOOD

PLY

MAGNET

HOLE COULD GET
FULL OF DEBRIS

OPEN

PROBLEM?

Easy

Yariv Sade, Arik Yuval/Igloo Design (2008)

www.igloo-design.com
info@igloo-design.com

The Easy water dispenser has been designed to hold three gallon and five gallon bottles of water. It includes the Green Tap Faucet, an easy system that prevents the tap from dripping and it functions in accordance with the laws of communicating vessels.

While the product name is Easy, its design was difficult. Not only did Easy have to exceed the success of its previous models, it also had to be affordable. Made using ABS (acrylonite butadiene styrene), Easy is durable yet also visual attractive.

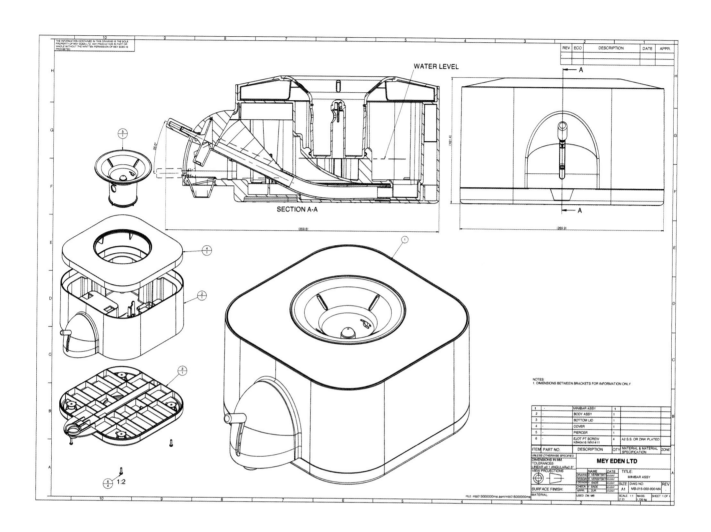

WATER LEVEL

SECTION A-A

A

A

NOTES
1. DIMENSIONS BETWEEN BRACKETS FOR INFORMATION ONLY

1	-	MINIBAR ASSY	1		
2	-	BODY ASSY	1		
3	-	BOTTOM LID	1		
4	-	COVER	1		
5	-	PIERCER	1		
6	-	EJOT PT SCREW KB40x16 WN1411	4	A2 S.S. OR ZINK PLATED	
ITEM	PART NO.	DESCRIPTION	QTY	MATERIAL & MATERIAL SPECIFICATION	ZONE

MEY EDEN LTD

TITLE: MINIBAR ASSY

SIZE: A1 DWG NO. MB-015-000-000-MA

1:2

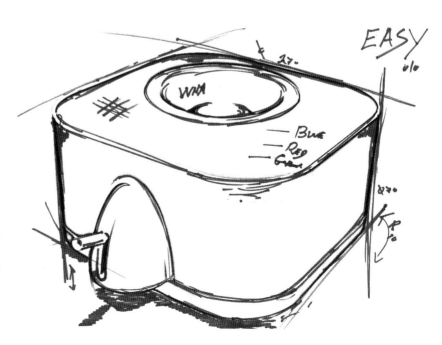

The sleek design of the Easy water dispenser and its ease of use make it functionally and visually compatible for every kind of work and living environment.

Etna Espresso

Mathis Heller, Gianni Orsini/WeLL Design (2005)

www.welldesign.com
info@welldesign.com

Etna Vending Technologies asked WeLL Design to design a complete range of automatic coffee machines. Over and above the technical redesign of the internal components of the coffee maker, WeLL Design had to cover the entire range of designs, from the most minimalist and cubist models to the more elaborate, featuring curved lines and sinuous silhouettes. The objective was to launch a wide range of products capable of appealing to any type of public. After a wide market study, WeLL Design created nine different coffee makers from a very minimalistic style to very emotional and curvy designs.

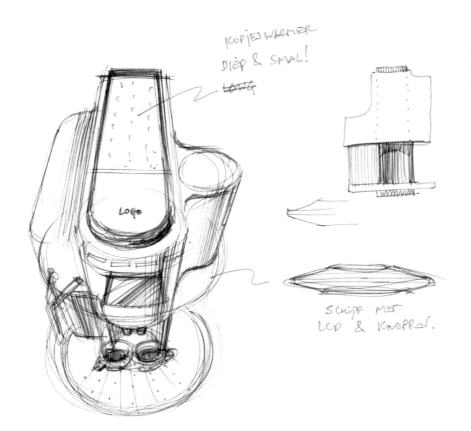

Sketches by Mathis Heller for Etna Espresso's design. Some of these sketches became the final prototypes of Etna Espresso's nine models.

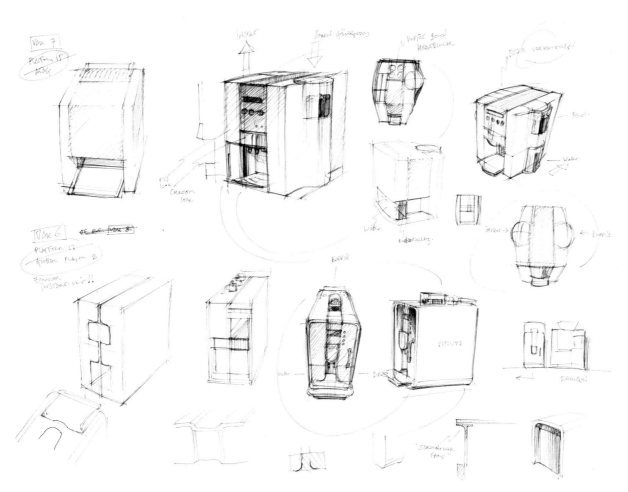

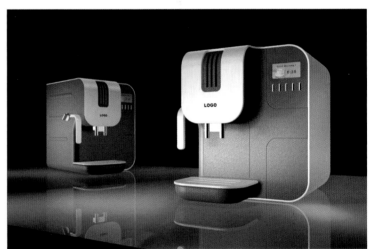

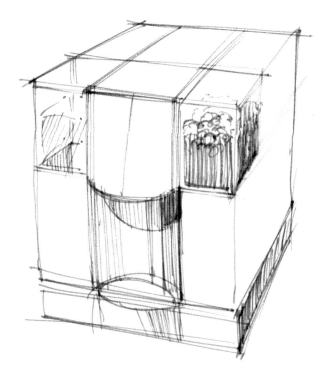

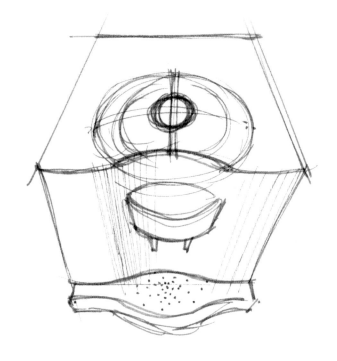

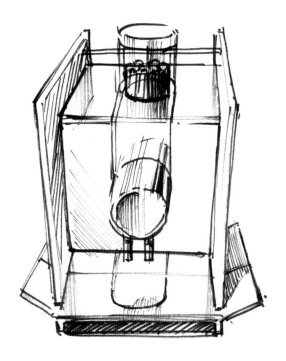

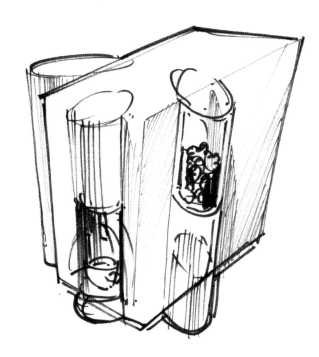

Preliminary sketches made by Gianni
Orsini for Etna Espresso's design.
Again, the sketches contain both
straight angles and curved forms to
explore all possible aesthetic options.

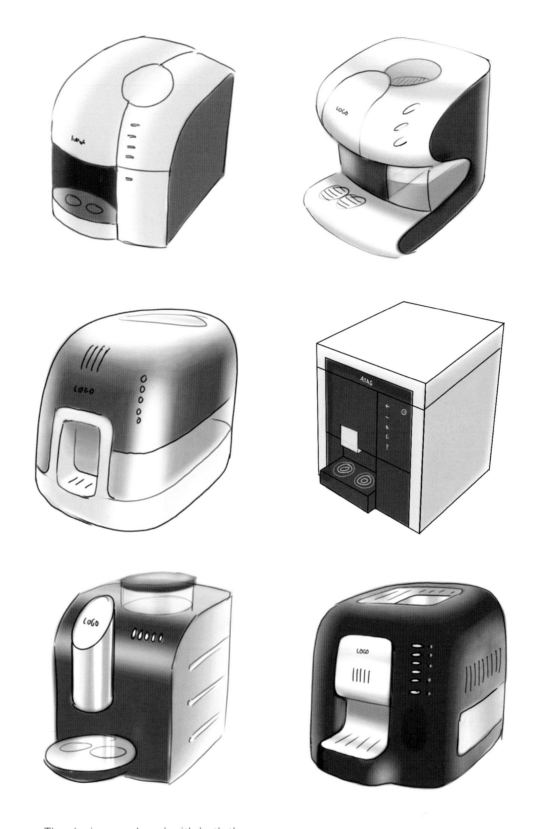

The designers played with both the silhouette of the machine and the positioning of the different elements, so that in some sketches these were integrated into the coffee machine and in others they protruded.

Folding Colander

Adrian and Jeremy Wright (2008)

www.designwright.co.uk
studio@designwright.co.uk

The Folding Colander, designed by Adrian and Jeremy Wright, can boast to be the flattest and easiest stored colander on the market. Built from one piece of polypropylene and available in several colors, the colander has twelve clips that allow it to be unassembled from its operative three-dimensional forms to its flat storable shape. Before coming up with the definitive design, 149 models were made over the course of several months before arriving on the final prototype. The colander won a Red Dot prize in 2008.

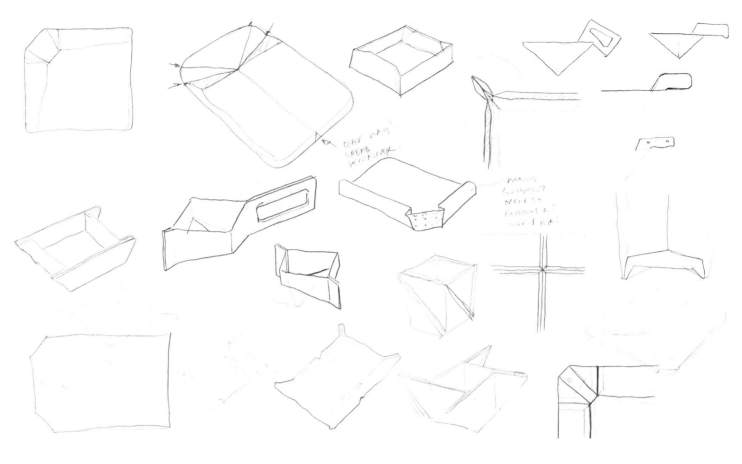

GAS

Adrian and Jeremy Wright (2007)

www.designwright.co.uk
studio@designwright.co.uk

The GAS stoves are a more flexible reinterpretation of traditional kitchen burners. The stoves can be used conventionally in the kitchen, but also individually in any other place in the home simply by connecting them to the electric network. The complete range includes conventional gas burners, a wok, a grill, a fondue set, stoves for coffeepots, and candelabras. After conducting several tests, a prototype was cast in aluminum and brass.

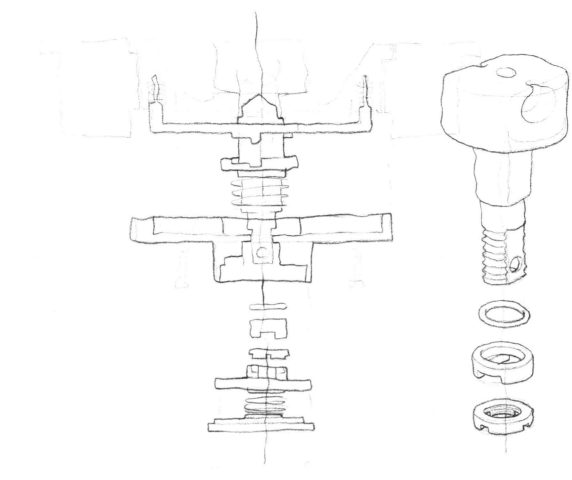

Gazelle

Designworks Windsor (2008)
www.designworksgroup.net
dw@designworkswindsor.co.uk

The Gazelle stapler has been designed with a steel body to maximize safety and durability. Gazelle has plastic ABS (acrylonite butadiene styrene) molds and rubber thermoplastic soft covers subtly integrated in the design to make it as attractive as possible. The stapler has a series of patented innovations, such as a loading indicator that warns the user when the machine is out of staples.

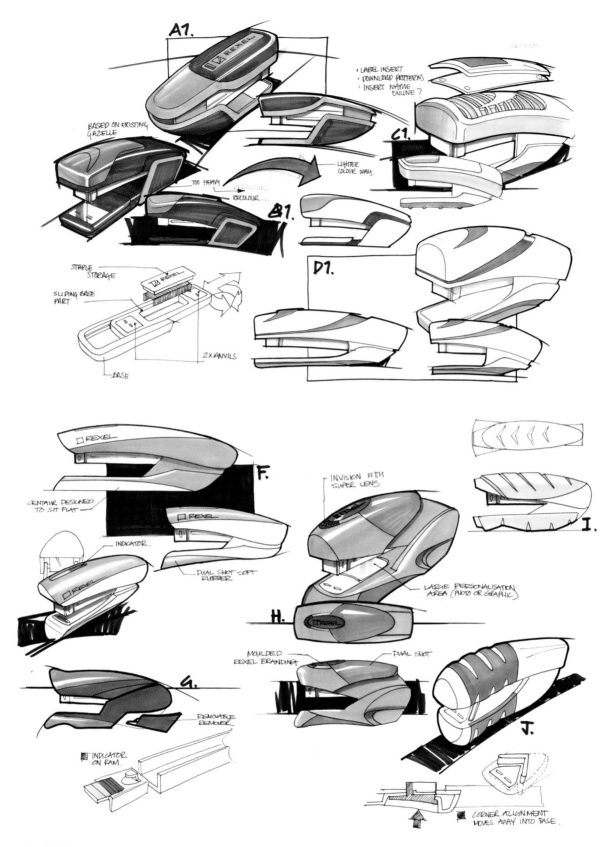

A1.

BASED ON EXISTING GAZELLE

TOO HEAVY

RECOLOUR...

RECOLOUR...

B1.

STAPLE STORAGE

SLIDING BASE PART

BASE

2 X ANVILS

· LABEL INSERT
· DOWNLOAD PATTERNS
· INSERT NAME ONLINE ?

LIGHTER COLOUR WAY.

C1.

D1.

REXEL

CENTAUR DESIGNED TO SIT FLAT

INDICATOR.

REXEL

DUAL SHOT SOFT RUBBER

F.

INVISION WITH SUPER LENS

LARGE PERSONALISATION AREA (PHOTO OR GRAPHIC)

REXEL

H.

I.

MOULDED REXEL BRANDING

DUAL SHOT

G.

REMOVABLE REMOVER

INDICATOR ON RAM.

J.

CORNER ALIGNMENT MOVES AWAY INTO BASE.

Preliminary sketches for the design of the Gazelle stapler showing the different options originally considered before settling on the final design.

InsideOut

BY:AMT (2007)

www.byamt.com
a@byamt.com

Photos: Lisa Klappe

The InsideOut collection by BY:AMT turns the natural order of things on its head. While each glass has a trapezoidal outline of a conventional exterior, its interior silhouette dictates what the glass should really be used for: wine, champagne, or a cocktail, for example. Functioning as a kind of negative of the conventional exterior, the interior silhouette of the glass is revealed only when liquid is poured into it.

DIK. VET

THICK
TO
THIN.

proporties.
dik + dun
groot & klein

SOLIDS.

groter + breder.

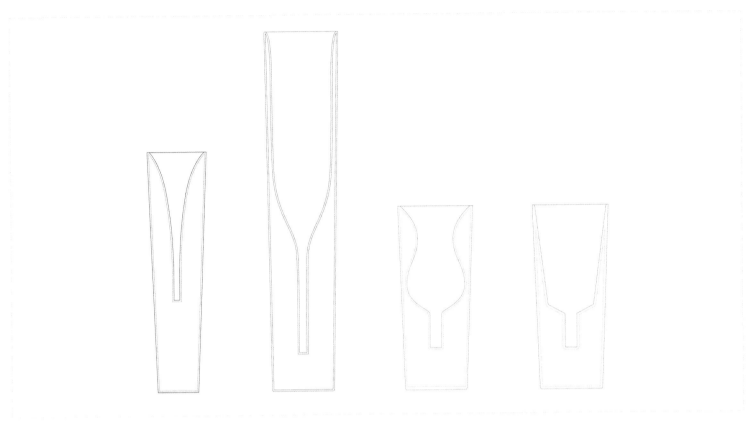

SIDE VIEW- More Or Less Glass NR. 3   SIDE VIEW- More Or Less Glass NR. 4

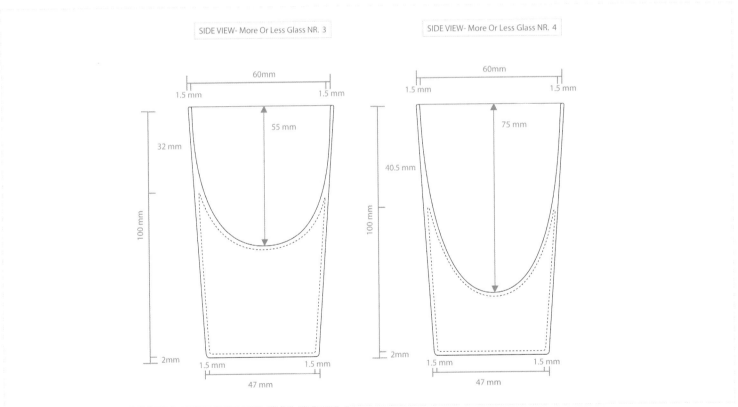

The idea of the "glass within a glass" has an additional practical advantage: the liquor inside is kept cold as the user's hand does not directly contact the wall of the glass.

kMix

Chris Christou, Johan Santer (2007)

www.youmeusdesign.com
mail@youmeusdesign.com

Kentwood is one of Britain's most well-known food preparation brands. Youmeus Design provided the impetus to steer the company into a new direction. With the creation of the kMix brand, Youmeus not only upgraded the products' design, but also developed new packaging and overall brand identity, transforming Kenwood into one of Britain's most hip food preparation brands, too.

These images are of early models and prototypes, which were used to explore visual language, configuration platforms, and performance.

The introduction of decorative patterns
is a way to add color to a product
category that, over recent years,
has been dull and sober.

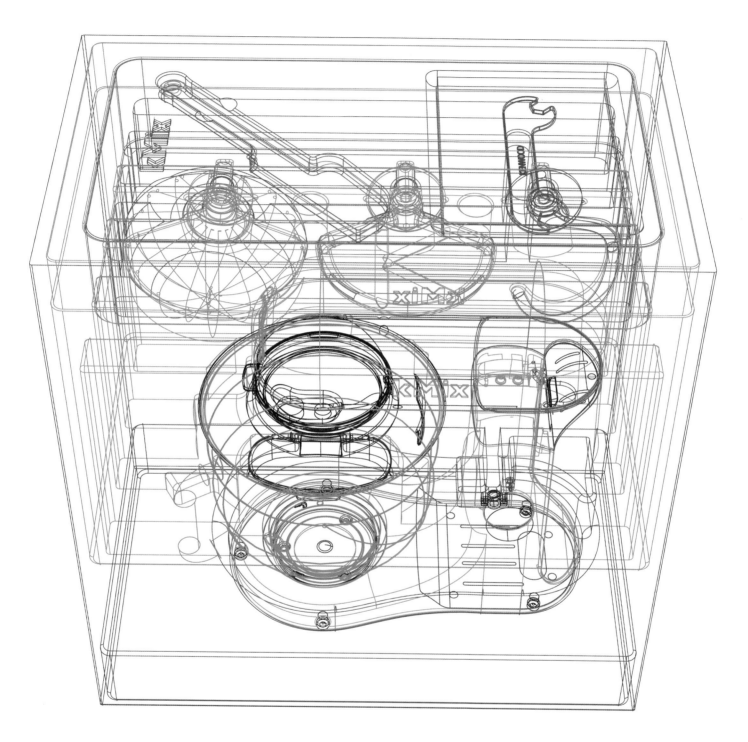

CAD (computer aided design) model of
the kMix packaging. Similar to opening
a jewelry box, the box consists of
several layers that lead the consumer
to its various contents.

LeChef

Anna Åberg (2007)
anna@aberg.biz

LeChef is a kitchen assistant capable of guiding the user, step-by-step, during the preparation and cooking process of a recipe. The robot is capable of memorizing and storing hundreds of downloadable menus. LeChef suggests suitable recipes for any occasion and the most suitable method to go about preparing them. Not only does LeChef centralize the user's recipe collection and avoids the accumulation of dozens of cookbooks, its human form is arguably much more interactive than a conventional book.

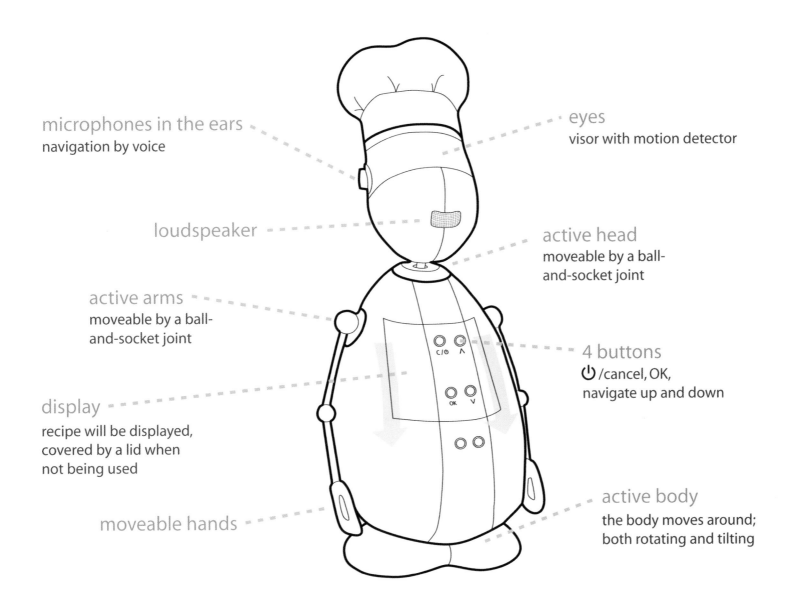

microphones in the ears
navigation by voice

eyes
visor with motion detector

loudspeaker

active head
moveable by a ball-
and-socket joint

active arms
moveable by a ball-
and-socket joint

4 buttons
⏻ /cancel, OK,
navigate up and down

display
recipe will be displayed,
covered by a lid when
not being used

moveable hands

active body
the body moves around;
both rotating and tilting

Medion Pod Espresso Maker

Myk Lum, Adam Wade/LDA (2008)

www.ldallc.com
mykl@ldallc.com

The Medion Pod Espresso Maker is an ultra-compact coffee maker that uses a 1.5 bar pressure system to extract the maximum possible flavor and aroma from coffee beans. With its double jet, the Medion Pod Espresso Maker can hold two cups of coffee, and has been designed to make changing the coffee loads as easy as possible. The large capacity deposit means that the water does not have to be changed frequently and its base surface area has been reduced so that it can be easily stored away. The side panels can be customized with different designs.

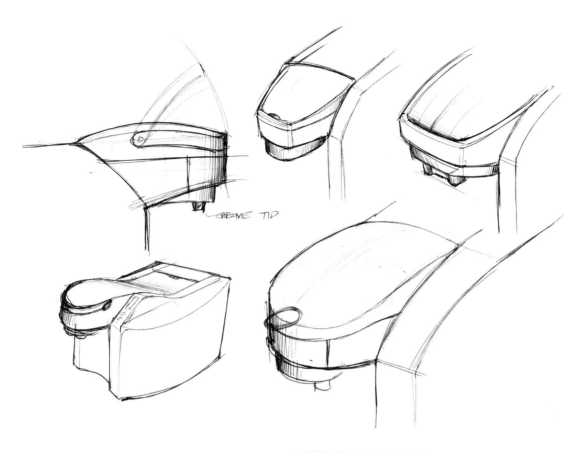

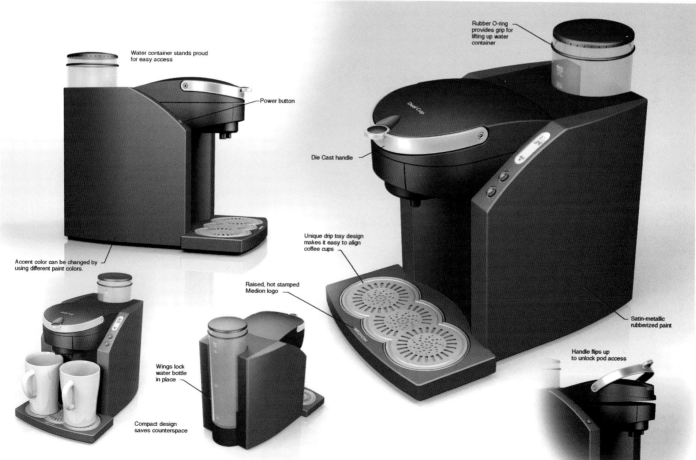

Water container stands proud for easy access

Power button

Accent color can be changed by using different paint colors.

Wings lock water bottle in place

Compact design saves counterspace

Rubber O-ring provides grip for lifting up water container

Die Cast handle

Unique drip tray design makes it easy to align coffee cups

Raised, hot stamped Medion logo

Satin-metallic rubberized paint

Handle flips up to unlock pod access

ME-ror

BY:AMT (2007)
www.byamt.com
a@byamt.com

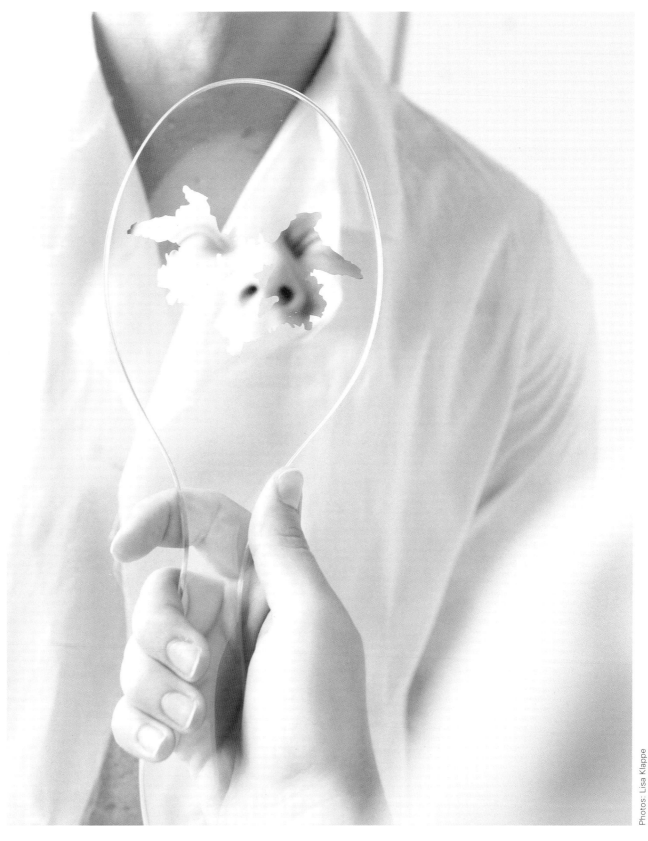

Photos: Lisa Klappe

The ME-ror mirrors by BY:AMT references Victorian times when women favored handheld mirrors. The viewer sees her reflection in one of three floating silhouettes—from a typical Roscharch test form to the profile of a woman to a plain oval. A modern take on an old classic, these mirrors have an ethereal quality, made all the more whimsical by the fact that the user must play with the angle of the reflection to get the best view of her face. BY:AMT is currently working on the wall version of ME-ror.

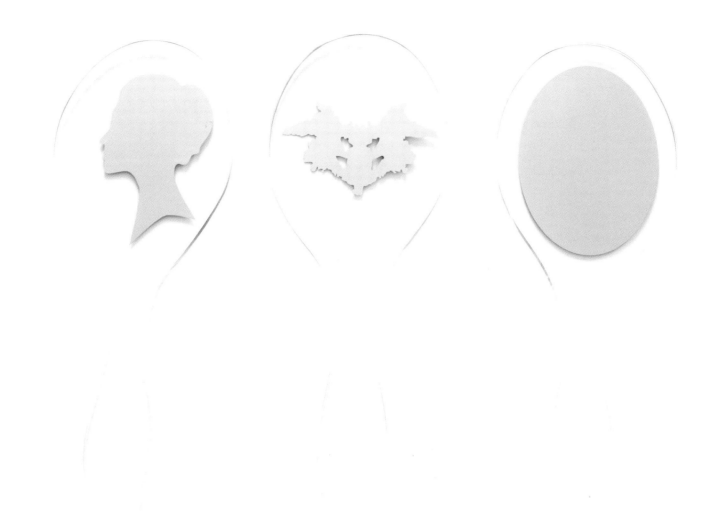

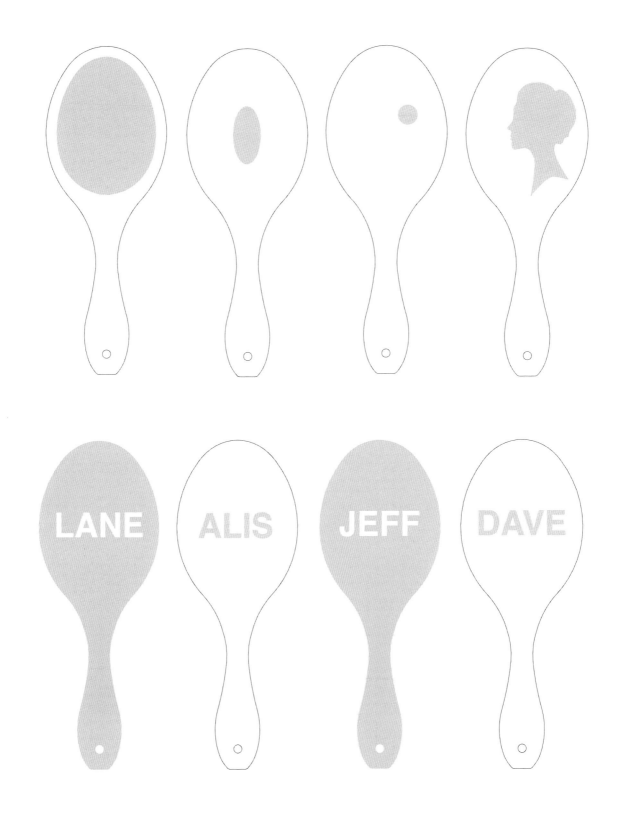

The names of the mirrors reflect the name of the user or anyone else, creating the paradox whereby the user is looking at an image in the mirror which may or may not correspond with the name etched on it.

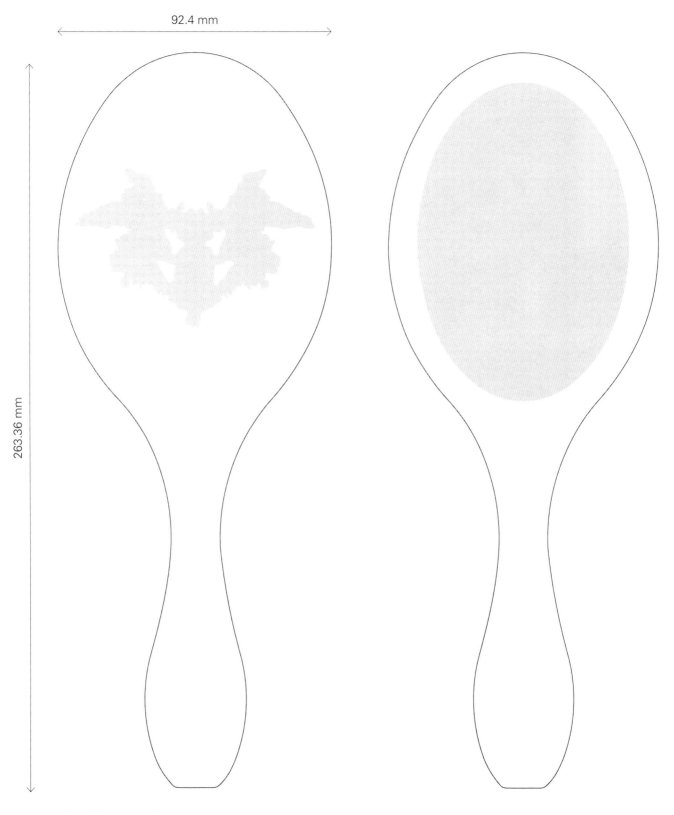

92.4 mm

263.36 mm

The different reflected forms which can be seen in the mirrors—the rest of the mirror is completely transparent—allow the user to see just a part of their face reflected: their eyes, their nose...

Office Desktop Accessories

Shaun Fynn (2006)
www.shaunfynn.com
info@shaunfynn.com

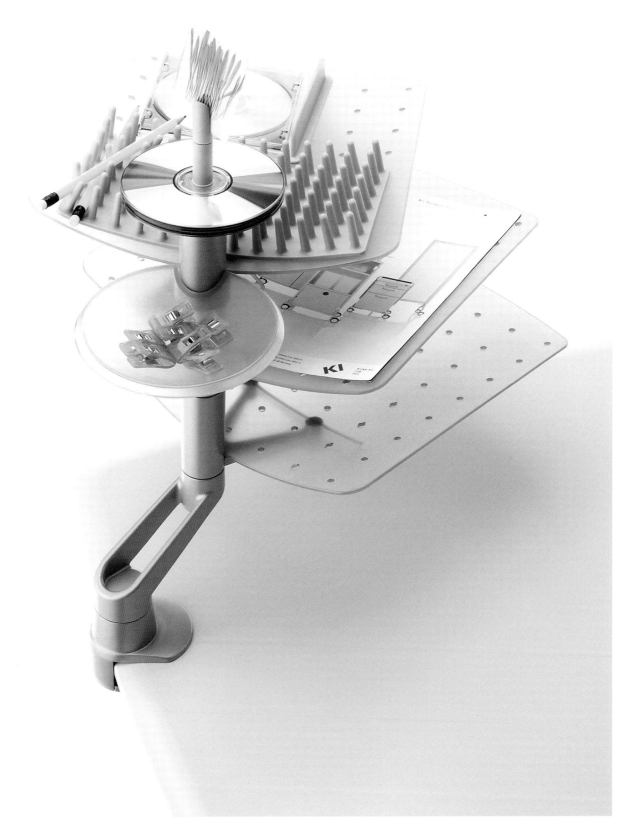

In an attempt to avoid the problems of a crammed and disorderly office, Shaun Fynn designed this system of trays that helps to organize and store paper, pens, and other office material. The system offers a compact, modular approach for any type of office configuration. The system can be mounted to the desk, and its rotating base and small reaching arm were designed for optimal adjustment, giving the user maximum flexibility for any number of uses.

Top sketch illustrates the myriad of ways that the trays and other organizational elements/pieces can be configured in the office workspace.

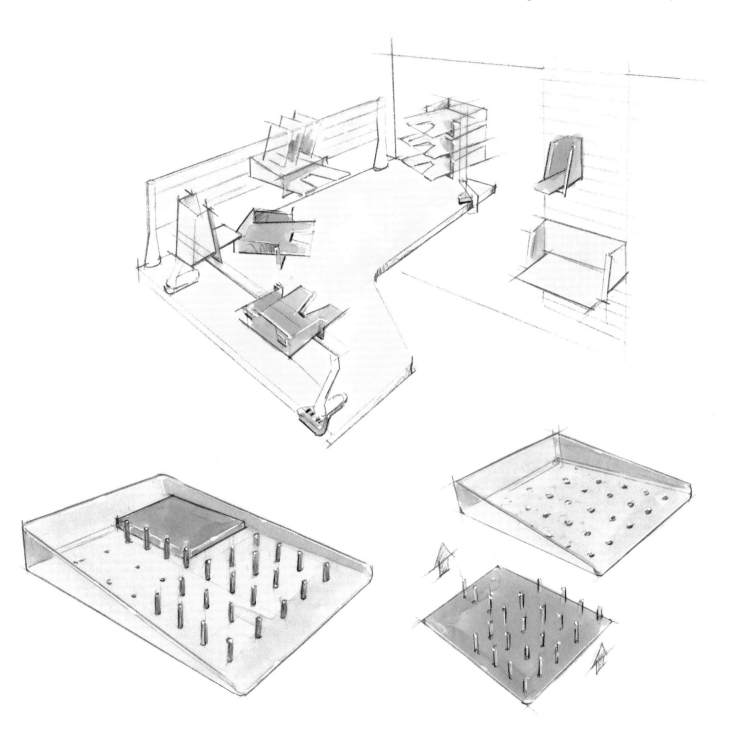

Bottom sketch explores the concept of a storage system where the user combines a mat with a tray where objects can be stored randomly.

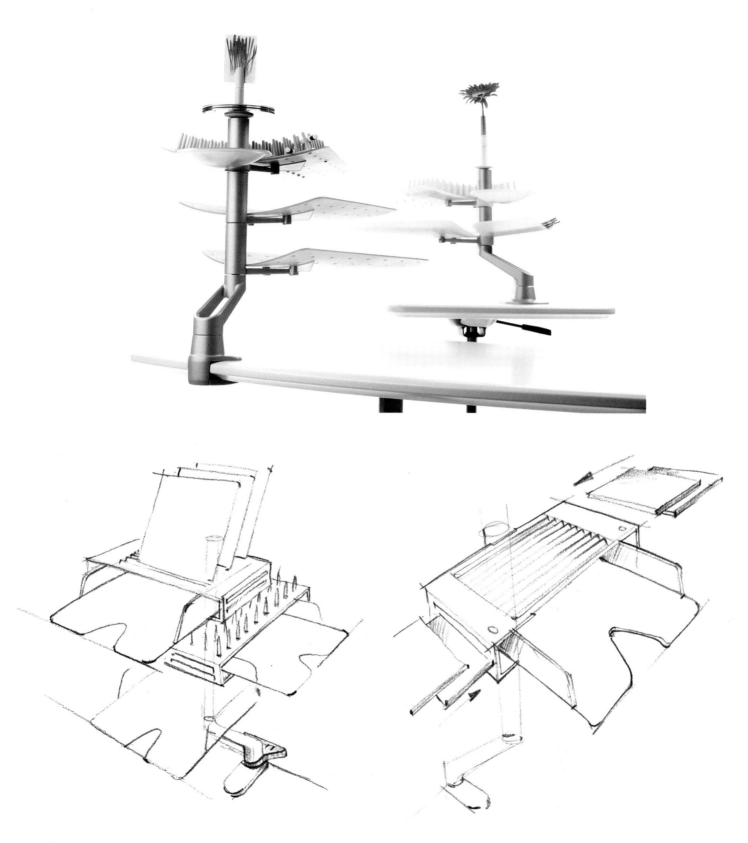

The base and the articulated arm are manufactured in aluminium; the trays are made from transparent plastic; and the yellow mat has been manufactured with a flexible, elastomeric material.

Detail shot showing the flexible elastomeric mats that are inserted into the trays to encourage the idea of non specific storage where the user can store things in a random manner.

Pebble Incense Burner

Shaun Fynn (2006)
www.shaunfynn.com
info@shaunfynn.com

The incense burner designed by Shaun Fynn is a contemporary interpretation of the traditional burners used in religious Asian rituals, adapted to the aesthetic tastes of Western consumers. The burner consists of two elements: a central aluminum piece, which holds the incense sticks and a concave space on the reverse, which holds the incense cones. The cherry tree wood base features space for holding extra cones and simultaneously collects the ash from the burnt incense.

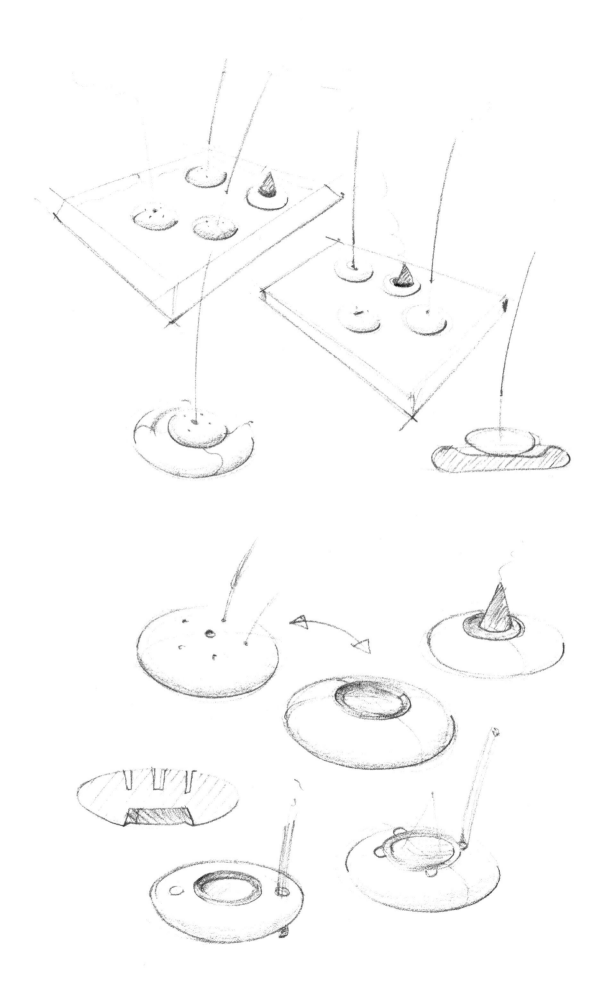

Princess Hairdryer

Mathis Heller, Gianni Orsini/WeLL Design (2006)

www.welldesign.com
info@welldesign.com

When the Princess brand decided to redesign many of their beauty and personal care products, WeLL Design stepped up the glam factor, putting Princess in contact with the high-end Swarovski brand. Swarovski suggested different ways to decorate the hairdryers with their crystals, all to stunning effect. The Crystal line is based on pre-existing hairdryers and includes three models: Crystal, Royal Bling, and Super Bling, lacquered in black and white.

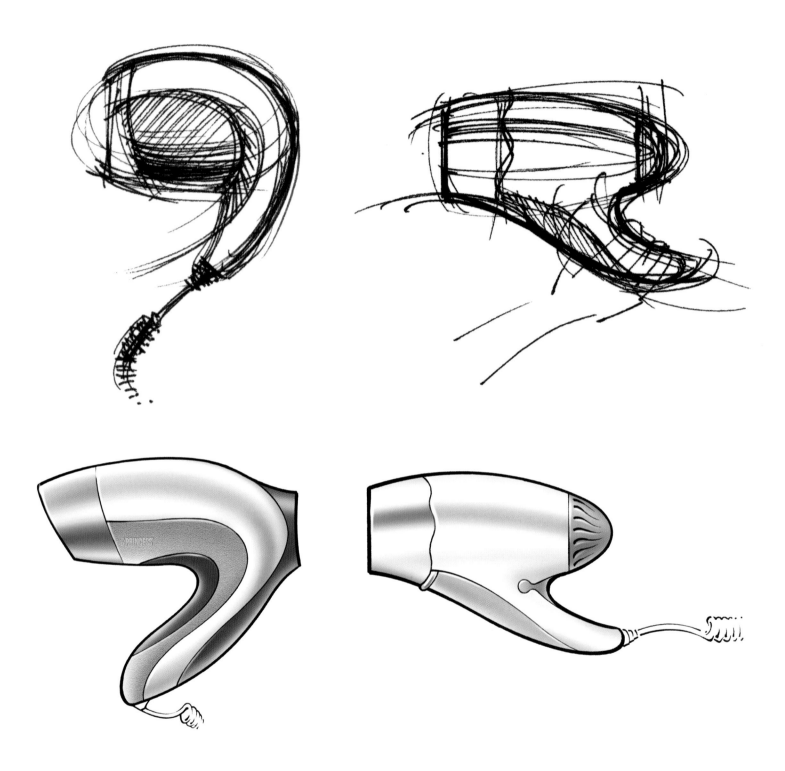

Not all of WeLL Design's ideas made the cut. The sketches seen here are of a prototype that never made it to final production.

The Racer stapler has been designed specifically for the French market. The design includes a loader, which stores the staples in the gadget's sinuous plastic covering. This cover is the main design element of the stapler and consequently the difficulty of this challenge. The redesign of Racer was based on an existing model to which plastic was added. The project was carried out in a short space of time and it made Acco, the manufacturing company, stand out among competitors in the saturated office material market.

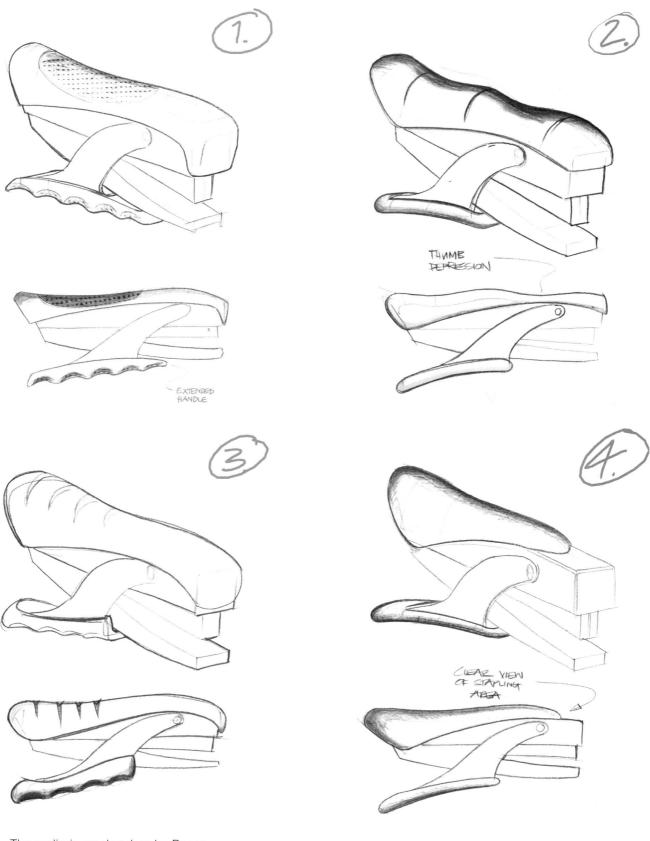

1.

2.

THUMB DEPRESSION

EXTENDED HANDLE

3.

4.

CLEAR VIEW OF STAPLING AREA

The preliminary sketches by Racer served to determine the best way of perfecting the stapler's grip. Different options were considered: rough and smooth surfaces, ergonomic forms, etc.

Smasher

Adrian and Jeremy Wright (2009)

www.designwright.co.uk
studio@designwright.co.uk

Smasher is a manual potato masher that, owing to its spring-loaded outer ring, captures the potato and forces it through the holes in the masher plate. For each step of the Smasher design process, a different prototype was developed. Each of the designs were individually tested until the designers reached the definitive model. Made from reinforced polypropylene (chosen because it is easy to clean) and stainless steel, Smasher is not only useful, but is also great fun.

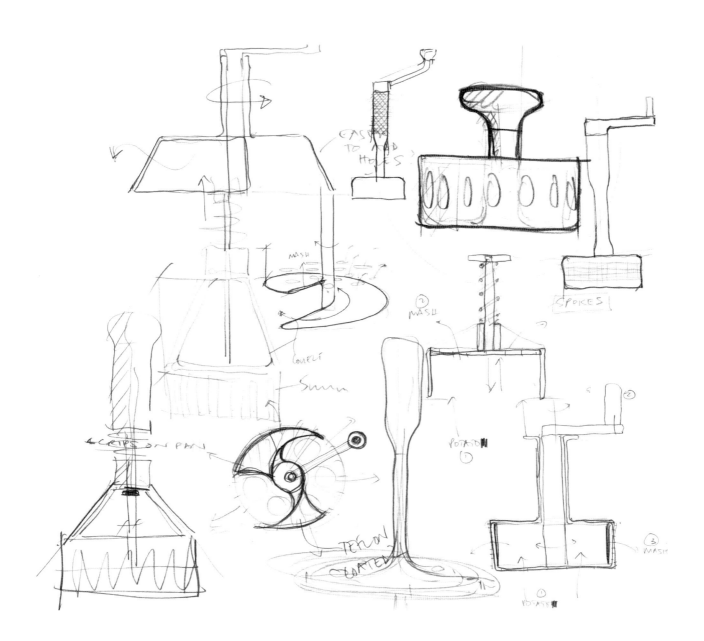

Steel Frame Dishrack

Adam Wade, Myk Lum/LDA; Frank Yang, Randy Wei/SimpleHuman (2008)

www.ldallc.com
mykl@ldallc.com

For this plate rack, the design team studied customer habits to understand the utenstil's use as well as the characteristics of modern kitchens. The results of their studies are seen here: the plate rack has stainless steel sides that help streamline the product's visual impact, allowing it to meld into its surroundings. Glasses are hung from the side hooks so as not to occupy space in the central tray, making this product as functional as it is fashionable.

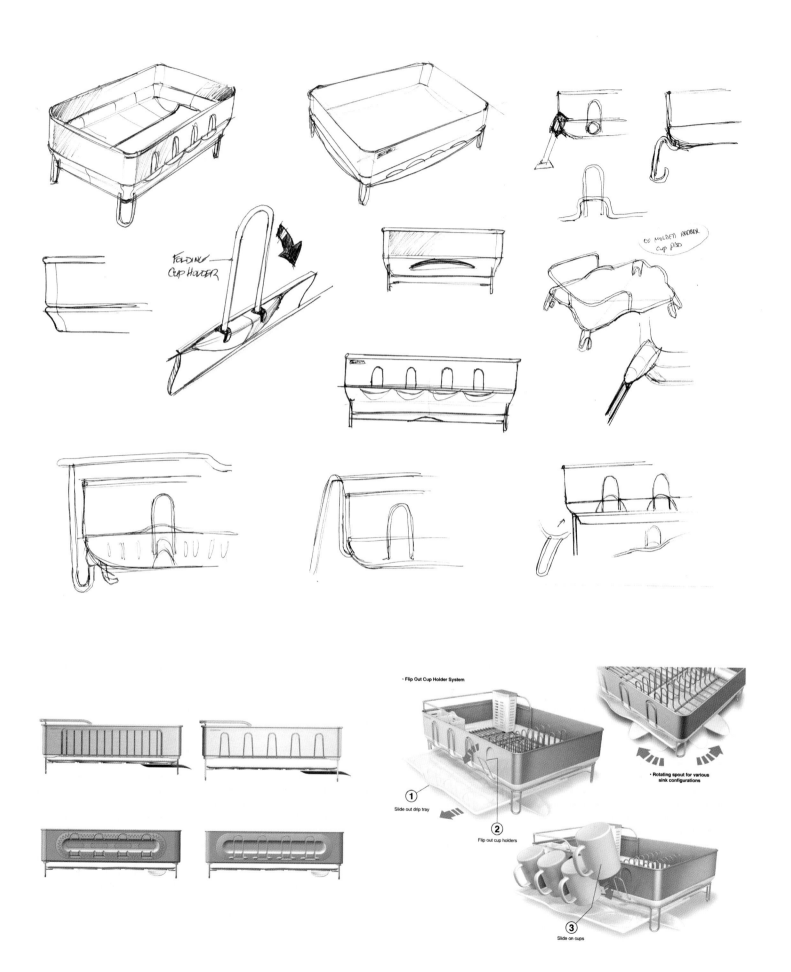

Folding
Cup Holder

co molded rubber
cup pad

• Flip Out Cup Holder System

① Slide out drip tray

② Flip out cup holders

• Rotating spout for various sink configurations

③ Slide on cups

Studies for Ballpoint Pens

Antonija Jurinec Campbell (2005)

www.keydesign.com
antonija@keydesign.com

After exploring an ideal ergonomic grip for writing, Antonija Jurinec Campbell has created dozens of ballpoint pen designs with an almost endless array of playful and attractive aesthetic possibilities. The refill for the ballpoint pen is both functional and aesthetic.

The materials used include foam, silicone, and rubber. Some of the ballpoint pens are knotted in the package, which adds an element of fun. Others, however, have been reduced to their minimum expression.

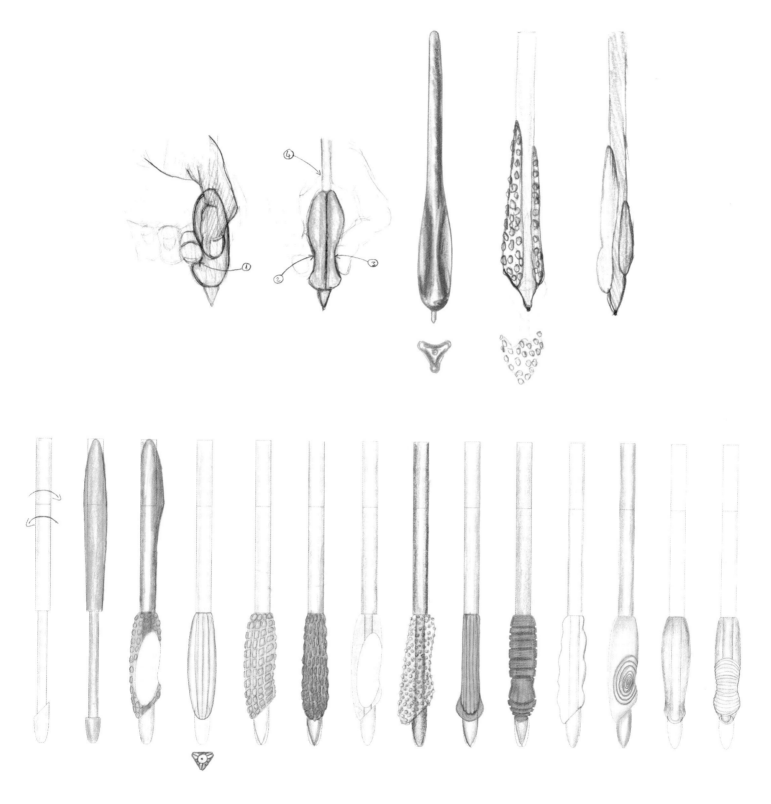

Ergonomic exploration led to an ideal triangular shape for the finger position. Some sketches include a bumpy texture for an improved grip of the ballpoint pen.

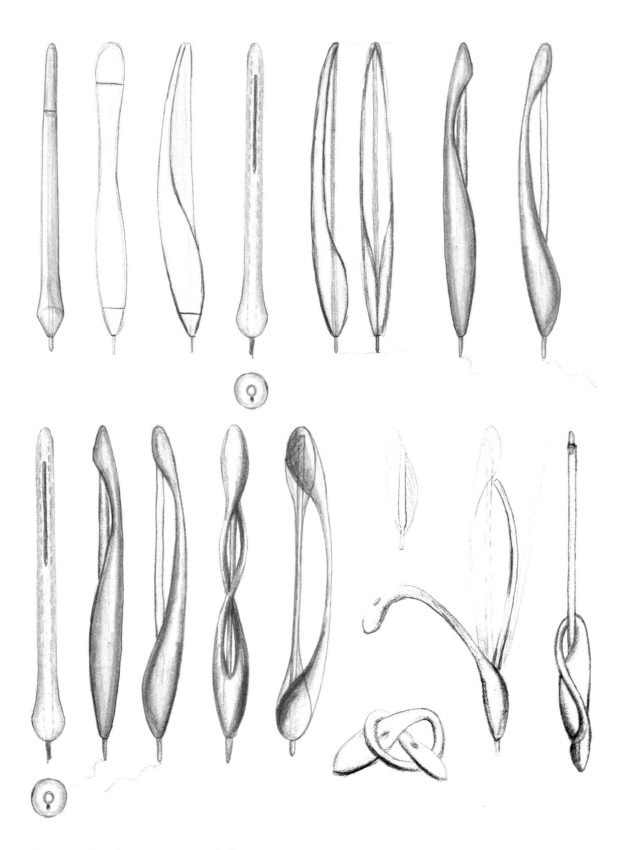

Some designs have an aymmetric form and others adapt to the user's fingers because of the rubber used on its head. The knotted foam can be untied to dress the pen refill, encouraging an element of play.

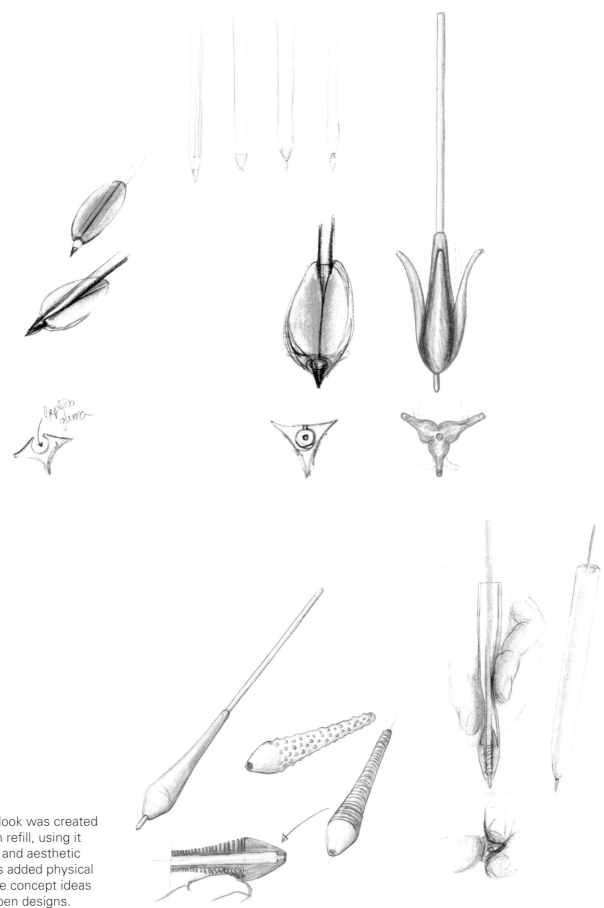

A playful and novel look was created by exposing the pen refill, using it as both a functional and aesthetic element. Prototypes added physical characteristics to the concept ideas and led to the final pen designs.

TicTac3

Yariv Sade, Arik Yuval/Igloo Design (2006)

www.igloo-design.com
info@igloo-design.com

TicTac3 is a magnetic clip with three legs that works on any metallic surface. But this product also has a special feature that sets it apart from other designs in the office material and stationary market: each of the legs is totally independent from the others. By simply applying a little pressure to one of the legs, the piece of paper is released without affecting the other two. TicTac3 is an evolution of TicTac2, the double magnet that won the IDSA design prize in 2004.

Tresdon

Jason Ivey/ICON Development Group (2009)

www.icondg.com
jason@icondg.com

Besides being completely ecological and manufactured with natural and biodegradable materials, Tresdon has an innovative design that takes into account the requirements and interests of both the distributor and consumer. The different elements that make up the bottle rack can be dismantled and assembled to build a wine box. No glue is required for assembly—the different pieces slot into each other perfectly. It is the perfect storage component for wine, whether carrying or displaying the bottles at home.

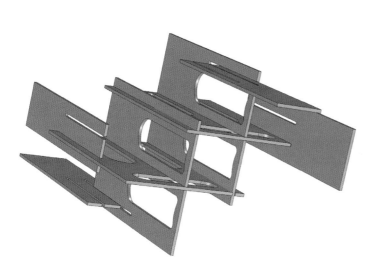

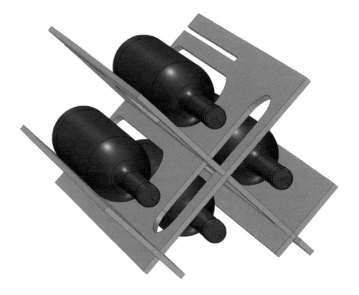

Tresdon, which is fully recyclable, has been designed to display its content and, in particular, the labels of the bottles. By adding modules, Tresdon can be as big or as small as the user wishes.

Vanishing Waterfall

Tom Korzeniowski (2007)

www.designdirective.com
tom@designdirective.com

The pump vault is one of the main elements of the Vanishing Waterfall system, an ornamental element designed for use in gardens. Manufactured in recycled polyethylene by a rotational molding technique—possibly the most used technique in plastic manufacturing—the Vanishing Waterfall can be produced relatively cheaply without hindering its capacities and functions. As cost-effective affordable as it is functional, this product is a model of affordable design.

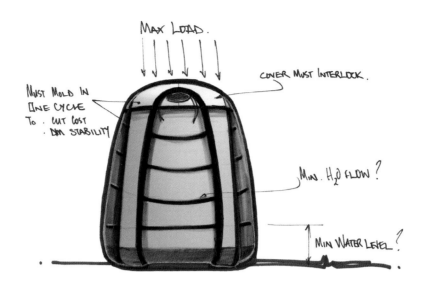

MAX LOAD.

MUST MOLD IN
ONE CYCLE
TO · CUT COST
· DIM STABILITY

COVER MUST INTERLOCK.

MIN. H₂0 FLOW ?

MIN WATER LEVEL ?

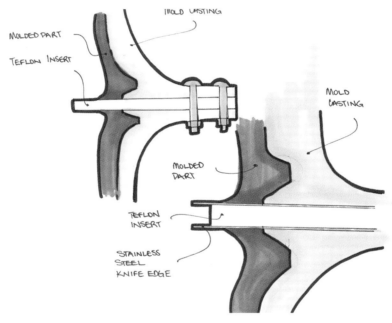

MOLD CASTING

MOLDED PART

TEFLON INSERT

MOLD
CASTING

MOLDED
PART

TEFLON
INSERT

STAINLESS
STEEL
KNIFE EDGE

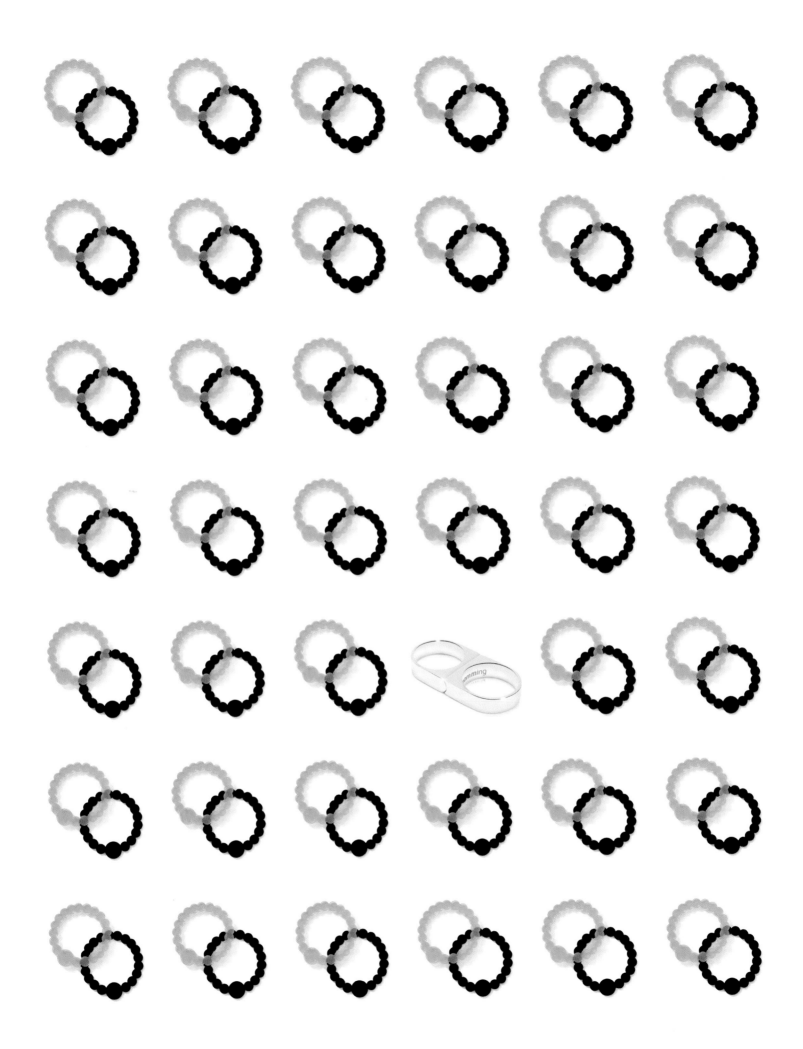

Sports Accessories and Fashion

Acme Made iPod Nano Clip

Brook Middlecott Banham (2008)
www.middlecott.com, www.brookbanham.com
brook@middlecott.com

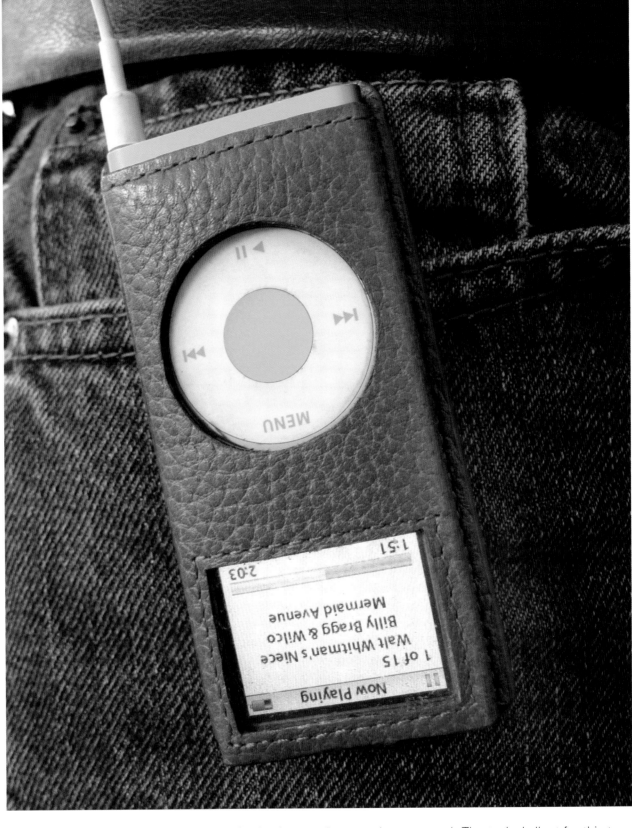

After selecting one of the many sketches for the Acme Made iPod Nano Clip, a prototype was developed in Illustrator and then the first trial models were manufactured. The cover is made from leather and has a steel clip so that it can be attached to the user's belt (or any other garment). The typical client for this type of product is someone who uses their iPod frequently and in particular someone who listens to music while doing physical activity.

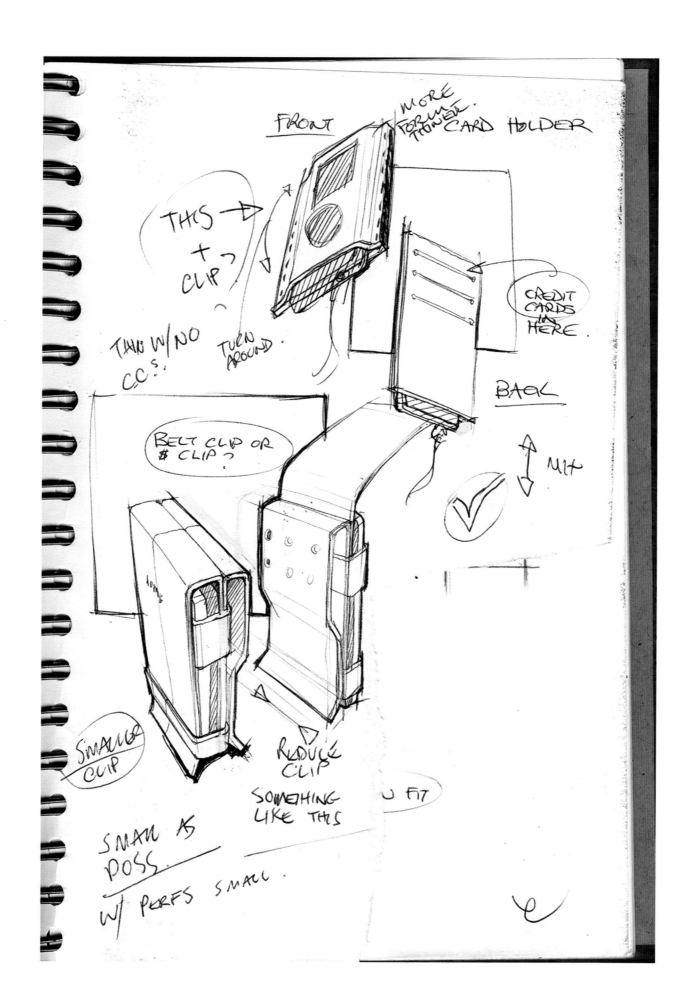

Acme Made iPod Nano Wallet

Brook Middlecott Banham (2008)
www.middlecott.com, www.brookbanham.com
brook@middlecott.com

The Acme Made iPod Nano Wallet was created to fulfill one simple desire: to create an accessory to store the iPod nano together with its headphones that would be as slim and functional as the Nano itself. The design team proposed several different sketches before arriving at the product design seen here. Available in three leathers—the perforated black saddle leather, the Tuscan orange or pink pebble grain leather, and a high-grade, coated leather—the model is updated with every new generation of the iPod.

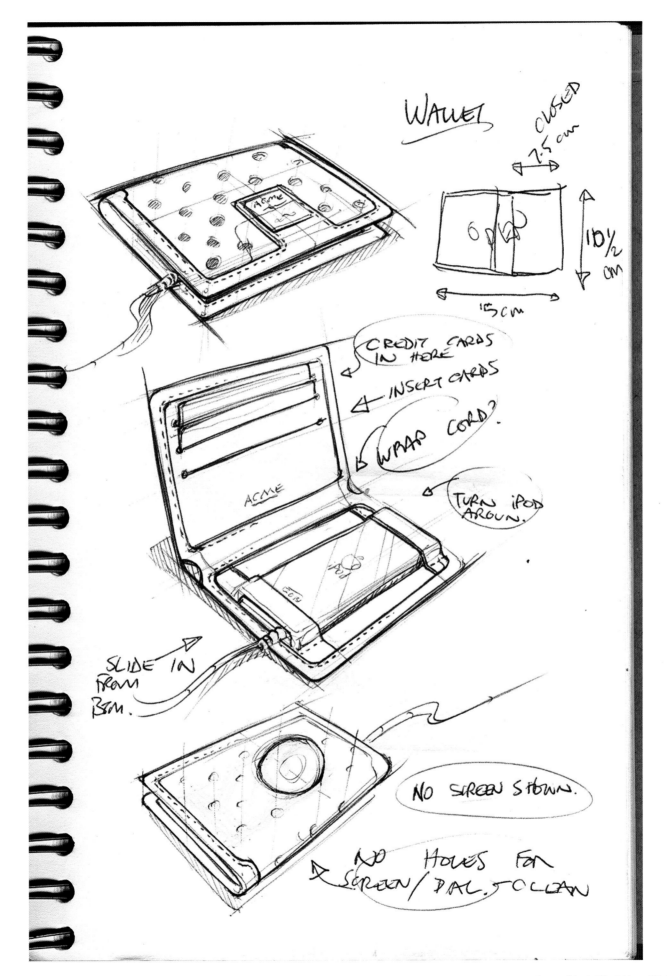

WALLET

CLOSED 7.5 cm

10½ cm

15 cm

CREDIT CARDS IN HERE

INSERT CARDS

WRAP CORD?

TURN iPOD AROUN.

ACME

SLIDE IN FROM BTM.

NO SCREEN SHOWN.

NO HOLES FOR SCREEN / DIAL. TO CLEAN

Acme Made Slim Pack

Brook Middlecott Banham (2008)
www.middlecott.com, www.brookbanham.com
brook@middlecott.com

Not all laptop covers are flat. On occasion, a design steers away from the traditional path and takes an innovative approach. In the case of Slim Pack's case, dozens of sketches were done before the designers settled on the model seen here. Made from leather, all of its components are carefully sewn, assuring maximum resistance and durability—comfortable, chic, and functional.

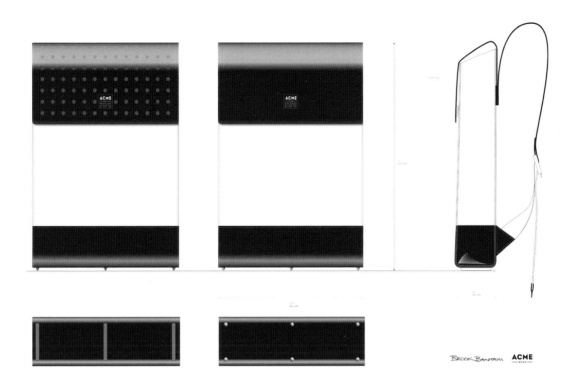

BROOK BANHAM   ACME

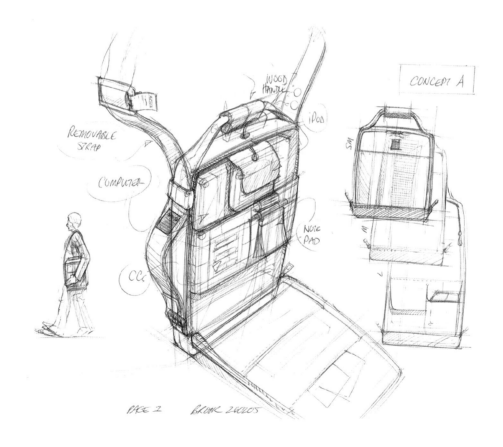

REMOVABLE STRAP

COMPUTER

CCU

WOOD HANDLE

iPOD

NOTE PAD

CONCEPT A

SM

PAGE 2   BROOK 260205

Adidas Quito

Jonathan Morss (2006)
www.morsfootwear.com
info@morsfootwear.com

The main objective in the creation of this product was to develop a fun, innovative, and resistant soccer shoe, something completely unique yet still functional. The first sketches moved away from the serious style associated with Adidas. As the project progressed, high-tech components of the shoe were accentuated without neglecting the organic details, which were adapted to a more Adidas-oriented profile. The end result is fresh and vibrant. The shoe is resistant and comfortable, yet stylishly singular with its asymmetric laces.

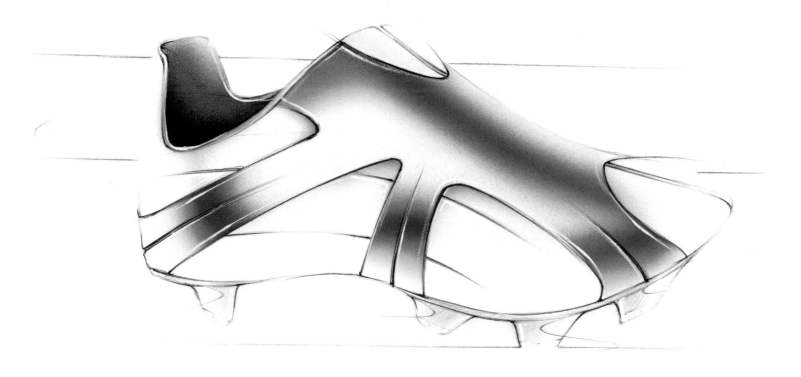

Balance

David Larsson (2007)
www.davidlarsson.com
david@davidlarsson.com

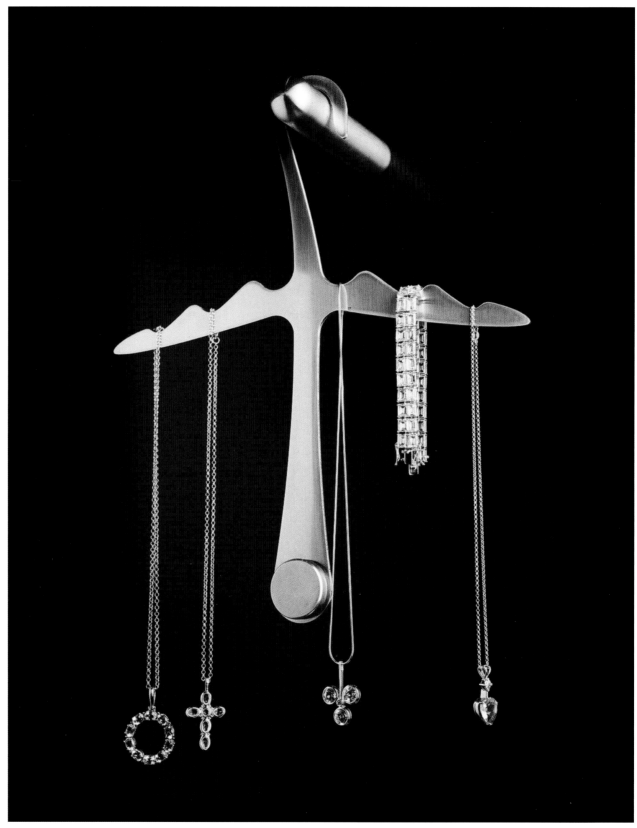

The Balance jewelry hanger is based on the notion that necklaces, bracelets, and rings should be on display, not hidden away in a jewelry box. In the preliminary sketches, the hanger looked more like a traditional hanger, and less like the finished design seen here. An intelligent counterweight system ensures that the hanger, made out of stainless steel, is always horizontal.

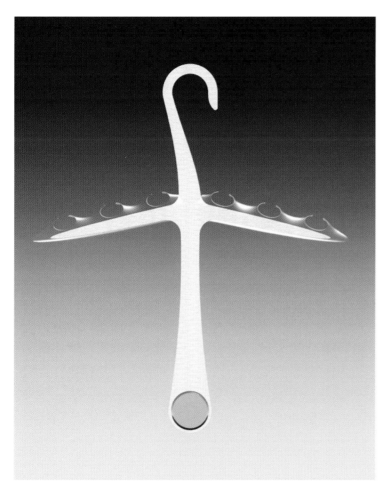

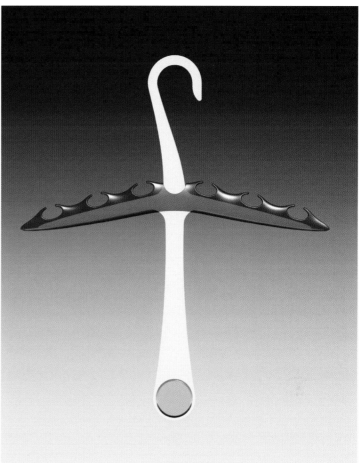

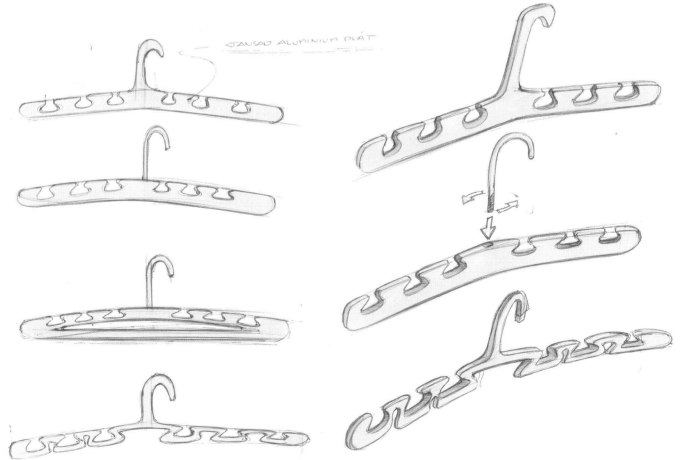

Birkenstock Birkies

Fuseproject (2008)
www.fuseproject.com
info@fuseproject.com

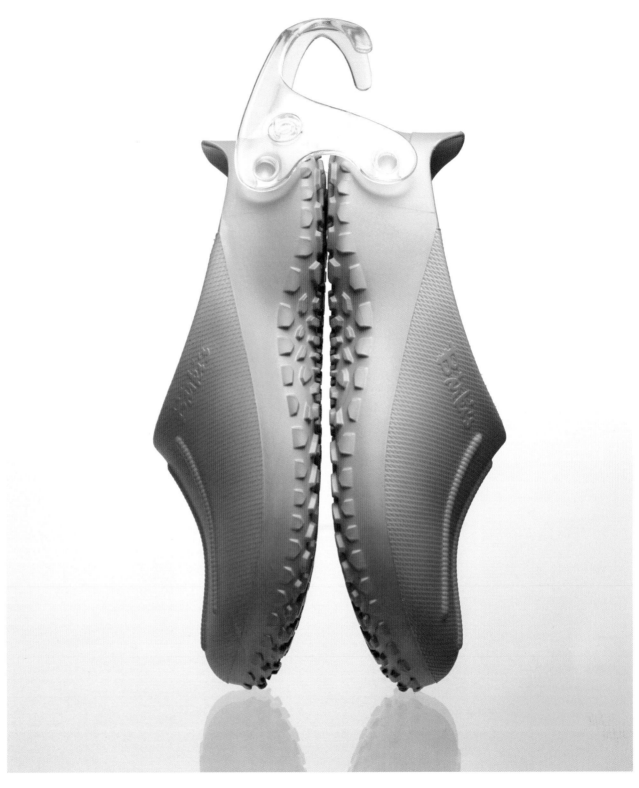

Fuseproject has worked with Birkenstock Birkies to create a new line of innovative products that showcase Birkenstock's overall brand evolution. The Birkies can be used both indoor and out, in professional environments and for leisurely activities. These slip-on clogs were specifically designed for the avid gardener, who works in both rain and shine. Their honeycomb patterned sole provides maximum slip protection and their built-in clip mechanism makes them easy to hang dry and store.

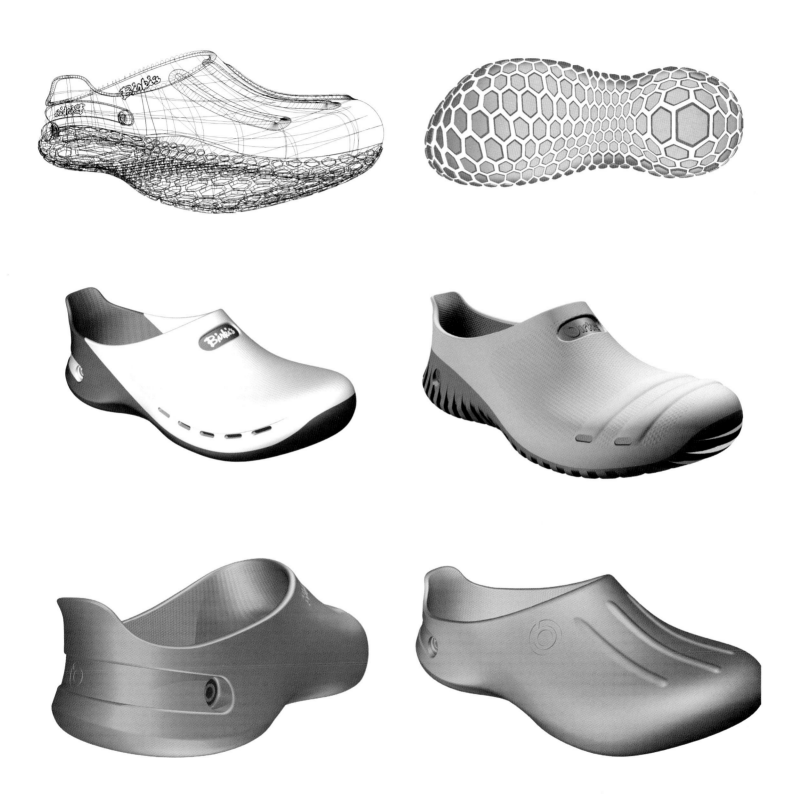

BMW MINI_Motion

Fuseproject (2006)
www.fuseproject.com
info@fuseproject.com

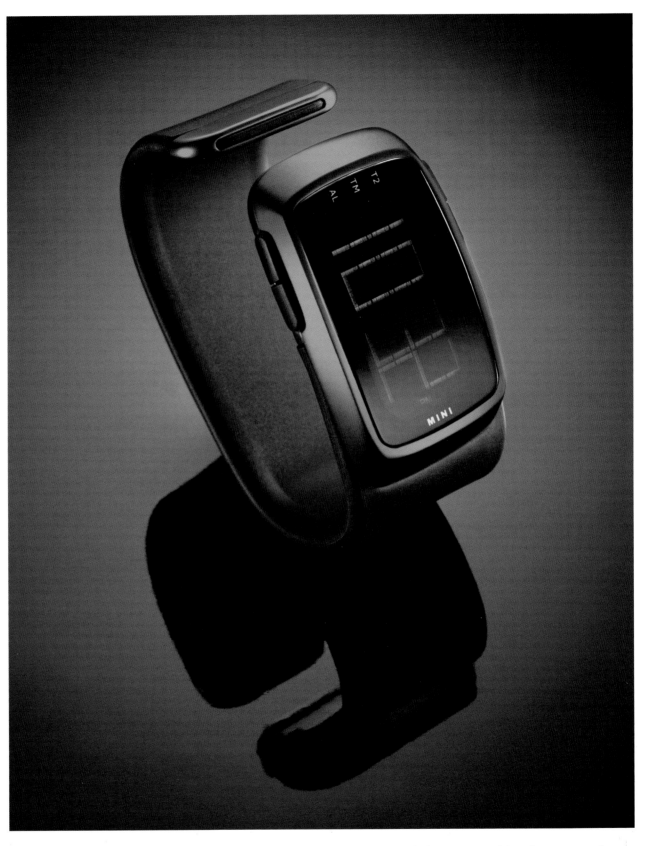

The collection of BMW MINI_Motion accessories (among them the wrist watches seen in this page) was simultaneously designed for the launch of the MINI Cooper and developed in collaboration with brands like Puma and Samsonite. Its objective has been to revolutionize the functionality of the products that are part of the range, taking "movement" as a conceptual starting point. BMW MINI_Motion also includes—apart from this line of products—the logotype and design of the packaging. BMW MINI_Motion both complements and extends the brand image of MINI Cooper.

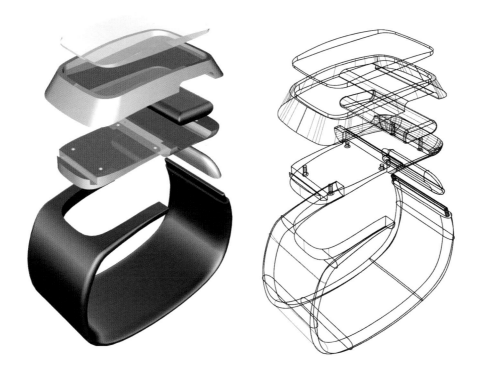

Co-developed by the British team Designworks Windsor and Dunlop, the ICE Dunlop Sports International racket sets a new standard of excellence in the world of tennis. Designed to emphasize and improve upon the power and control of the shot, the molecular structure of the racket has been reinforced during the manufacturing process to give it a lighter, more manageable body. Not only is the racket technologically advanced, but it also is ergomically balanced—from the design of its head to the structure and detail of its handle.

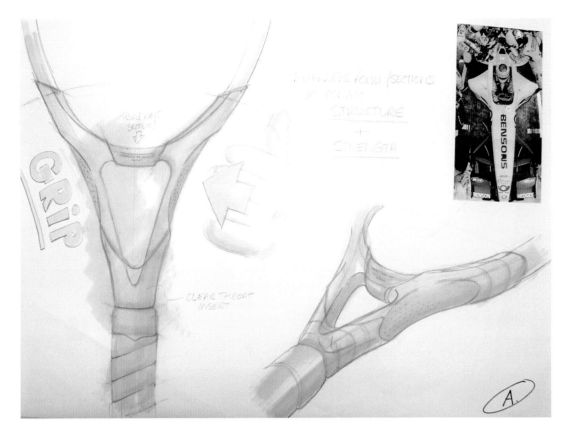

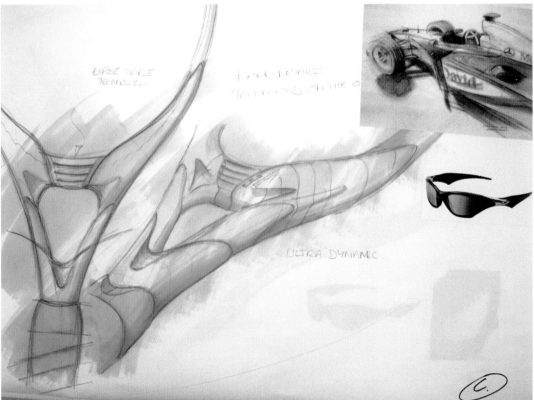

Previous design sketches done by the designers. The design is inspired by modern sports equipment. Head form and tactile neck detail compliment the ergonomic form.

Involution, Split and Zaeta

Jason Farsai (2008)
www.jasonfarsai.com
jasonfarsai@gmail.com

SPL/T

These three billiard table designs evolved from inspirations ranging from nature to transportation to architecture. Their structures, materials, and configurations are unique to the market. Each is innovative in its own ways, and was designed to evoke emotion through form and function. The designs are sleek and stylish, and are meant to target a previously untapped market segment. It was crucial for the designer to keep a realistic approach, while pushing the boundaries at the same time.

BILLIARD TABLES

INVOLUTION: 1. THE ACT OF BEING INVOLVED
2. INTRICATE
3. AN INWARD CURVATURE OR PENETRATION

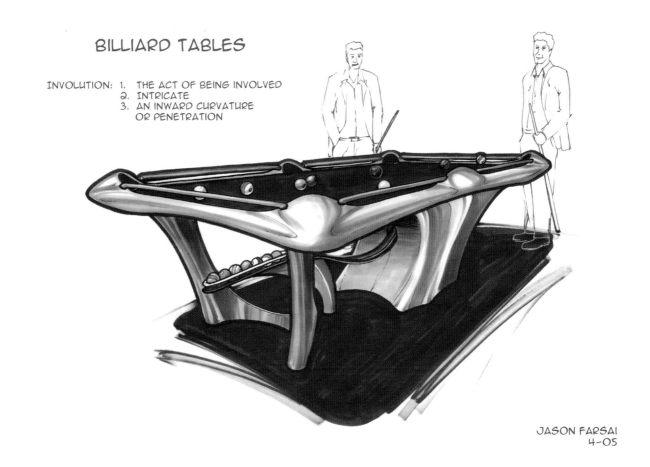

JASON FARSAI
4-05

In Jason Farsai's words, "the Involution billiard table combines the styling cues of the exotic Bird of Paradise Flower and the stylish Bugatti Veyron sportscar."

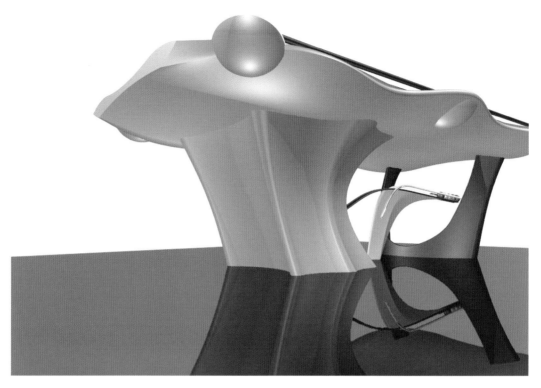

These 3-D renderings graphically
illustrate the design's seamless form
and how it breaks the classic straight
lines of traditional table.

Jason Farsai's senior thesis was titled "Beyond Billiards," and nothing more accurately captures that sentiment than the design of Zaeta. Seen here in model form, the table's name references the Z-shaped form of the table's base.

Jewelry Collection

BY:AMT (2003)
www.byamt.com
a@byamt.com

The jewelry collection designed by BY:AMT brings to mind the fairy-tale jewelry of old Hollywood movies, although in a low-budget version and made using materials much less expensive than gold and diamonds. The wide range of colors available in rings such as medals, bracelets or necklaces adds a touch of significance to the pieces: red is passion and strength, green is health and youth, while yellow in some cultures represents infidelity and jealousy.

1.5"

The plastic medals are inspired by traditional sporting awards, and also by the heraldic designs of military badges, with this individual symbolism.

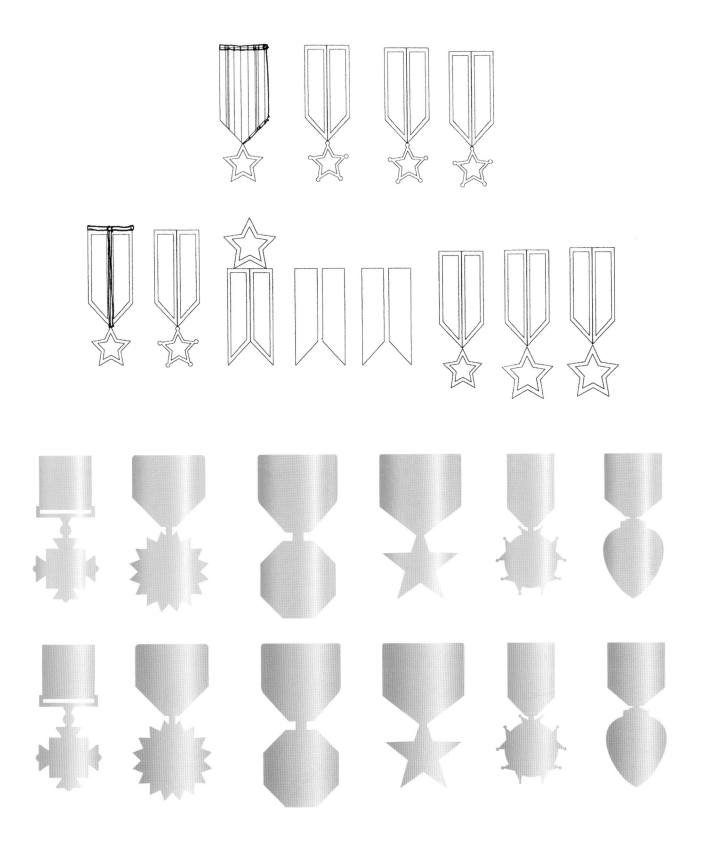

BY:AMT plays with the size and colors
of the medals, with the objective being
that the user combine the different
pieces of the collection in creative
and unusual ways.

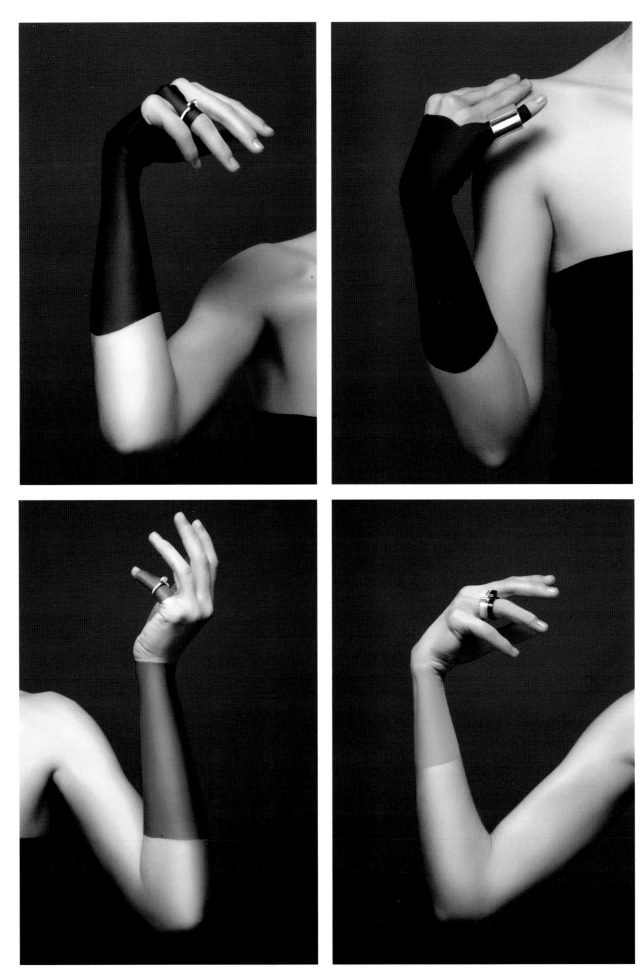

The jewelry range BY:AMT is an ironic reflection on the human obsession for symbols of power and social position. BY:AMT jewelry invites us to take a step back and have a laugh at our own expense.

Living Range

Michael Young (2008)
www.michael-young.com
contact@michael-young.com

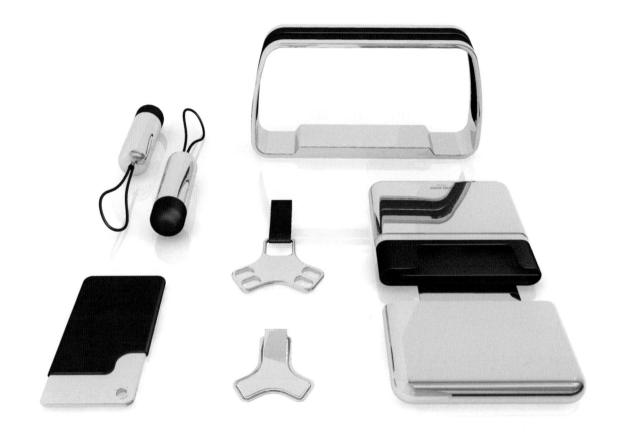

Designed for the frequent traveler, the Voyage family of accessories, manufactured in stainless steel, is comprised of a document holder for travel documents, like a passport, an individual keyring, and a suitcase identifier in the shape of a cylinder that holds a card with pertinent travel information. There's even room for a pen. Enclosed by a black polycarbonate lid, the Living Range is both elegant and minimalist. The family of accessories is sold separately.

Puma Tempo

Edgar Guillen (2006)
www.ydeaz.com
info@ydeaz.com

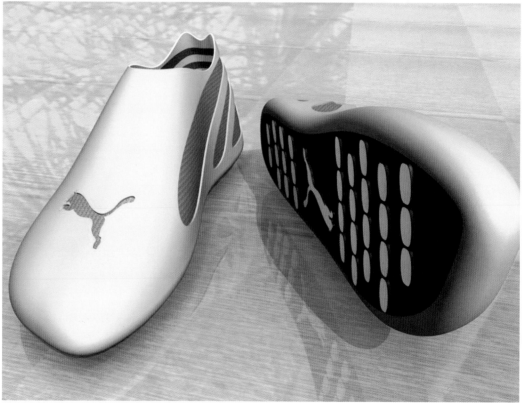

The sneaker model Tempo by Puma has been designed with the concept of "freedom" in mind: freedom of movement and freedom of action. The idea behind the design is that the user should forget that they are wearing shoes and, instead, feel as though they are floating on air. The Tempo sneakers regulate the wearer's temperature and are totally sustainable and ecological, as they do not use glue in any of the elements and they have been manufactured with pine fabric, a material used frequently in textile with silk and polyester.

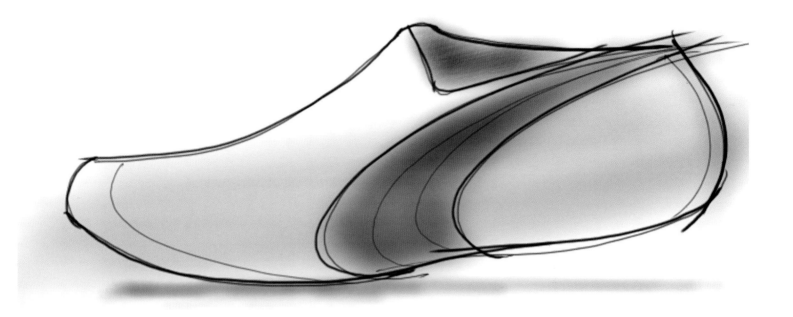

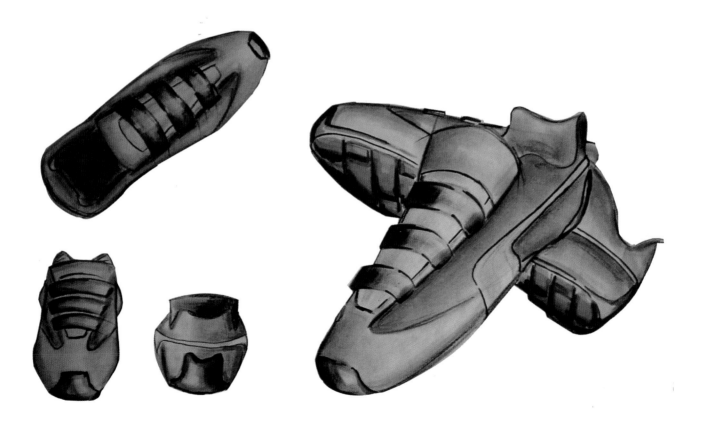

Ring-A-Day

BY:AMT (2005)
www.byamt.com
a@byamt.com

A different ring for every day of the week. This is the concept on which the Ring-A-Day family of rings is based. They are die cast in either silver or stainless steel plaques in groups of seven, one for every day of the week. The user only has to separate them from the sheet and polish the edges with the sandpaper enclosed. Once die cast and polished, the individual plaque that holds it can be used as a pendant or even as a decorative element for the wall.

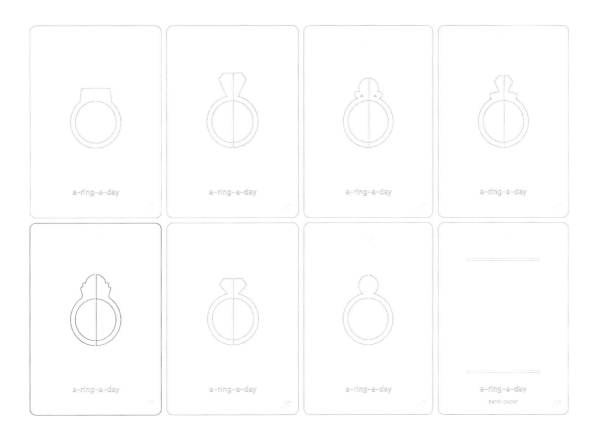

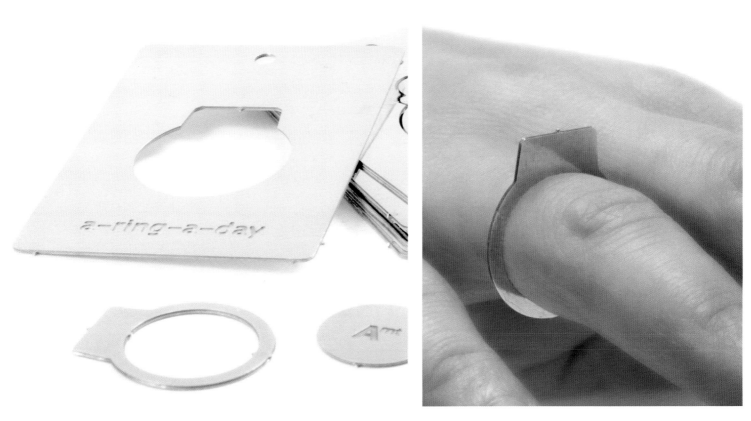

The Ring-A-Day collection is a paradox in itself. Which is more valuable—the ring or the sheet?

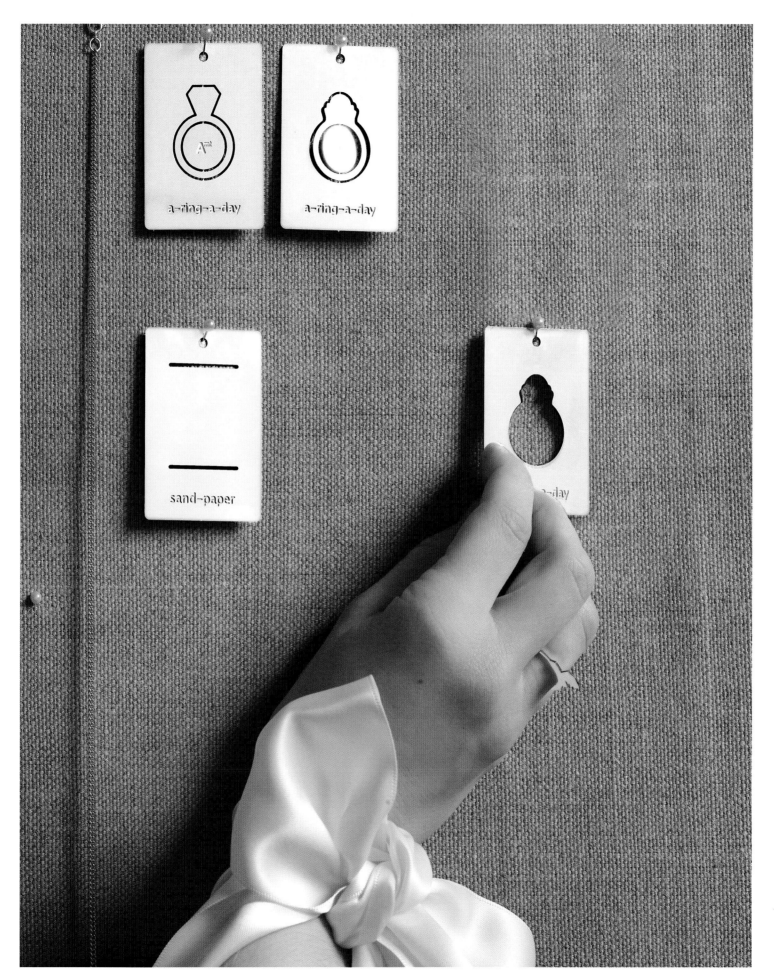

Ringset ONE

Bas van Leeuwen, Mireille Meijs (2008)

www.bloomming.com
info@studiobloomm.com

Ringset ONE is a set of two practically identical, minimalist rings, but with special feature that sets them apart: the base of one of the rings has a slight convex curve while the other has a slight concave curve.

Both rings perfectly fit into each other at the base, bringing to mind the concept of duality as expressed in its most artistic form.

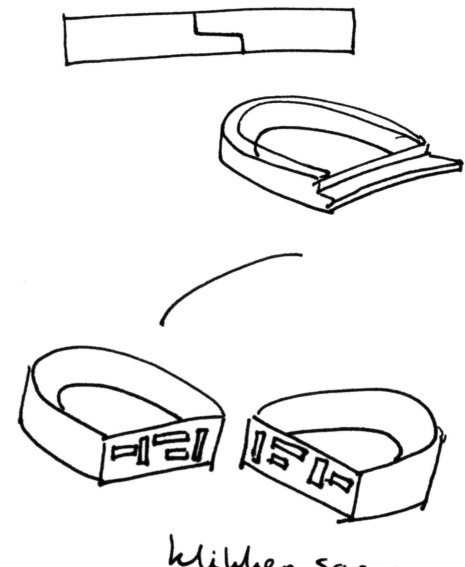

klikken samen

Sketches for Sneakers

Brook Middlecott Banham (2008)

www.middlecott.com, www.brookbanham.com
brook@middlecott.com

BROOK 060901

These sketches, by Brook Middlecott Banham, are case studies for experimental prototypes of sneakers. Each sneaker has an innovative design element. The sneaker seen above, for example, uses liquid both as a shock-absorber filling element and as a cooling mechanism. The sneaker seen on page 172 uses polymeric flaps as an alternative to the traditional shoelace.

HANDMADE ITALIAN SHOES-
-NO MOLDINGS
-EMBROIDERY-HEAVY USE
SCREEN PRINTED LEATHER
-HIGH QUALITY
ITALIAN LEATHERS

EMBROIDED LOGO

Michael Schu...

FILA

CONCEPT LOWER DENSITY EVA HERE.

EMBROIDERED DETAILS

LOWER CUT

EMBROIDERED LOGO

FILA

GRAPHIC DETAIL

UNKNOWN MATERIAL

EXHAUST

FILA

FILA

CUT MIDSOLE FOR COLOUR BLOCK

CONCEPTS-SCHUMACHER B/POOR SHOE

...SKETCHES

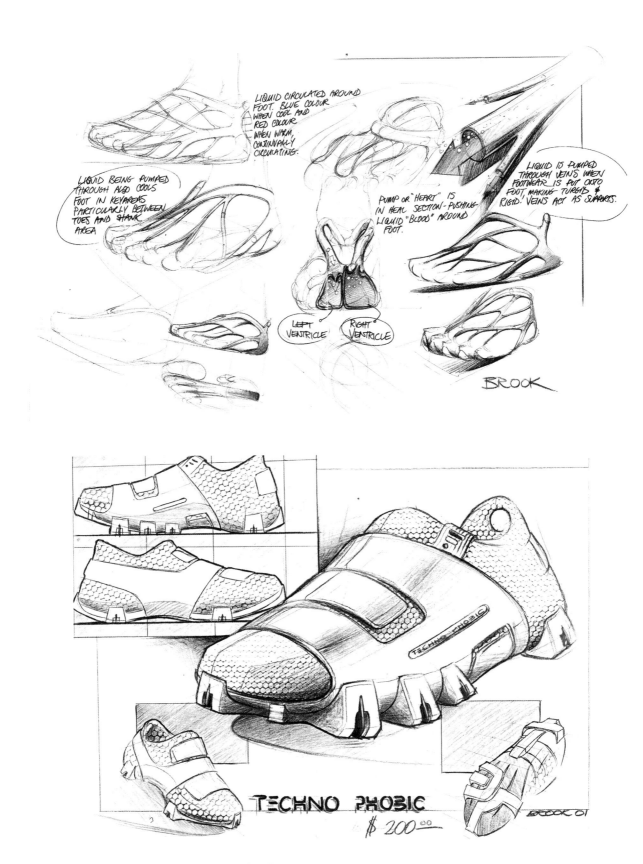

Banham found his inspiration for these designs from a variety of sources, including the silhouette of a shark for the shoe seen on page 173.

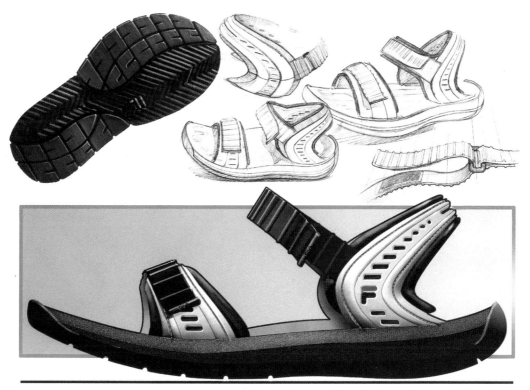

BROOK

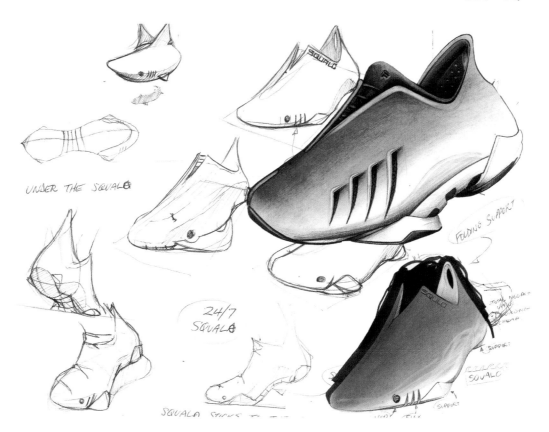

UNDER THE SQUALO

FOLDING SUPPORT

24/7
SQUALO

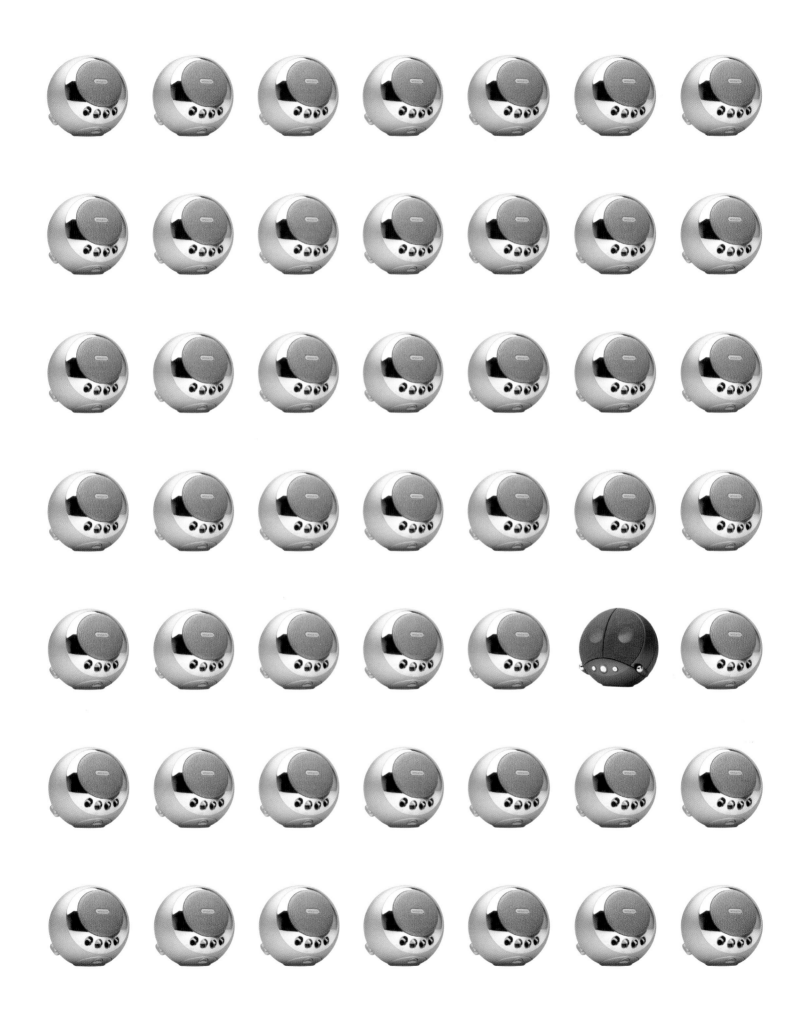

Technical Gadgets and Toys

3YE

Eschel Jacobsen (2008)
www.eschel.com
jacobsen@eschel.com

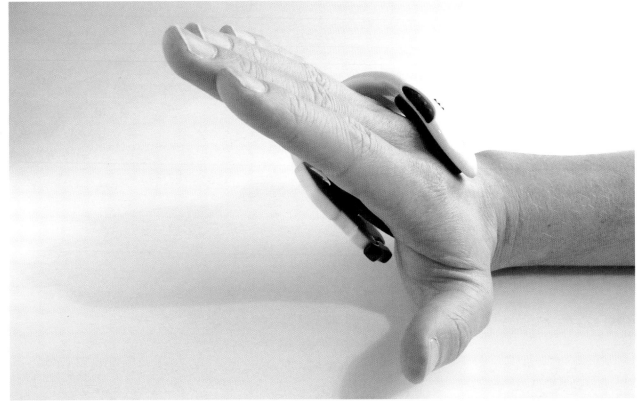

3YE (third eye) replaces the walking stick by transforming visual input into physical information, creating a tactile vision for blind people. With 3YE, it's possible to record a route and be guided physically by this information if the user wants to go to the same destination again. It was the designer's goal to strengthen the user's non-working senses, but it was important that this shouldn't weaken working senses, like hearing, smell, etc. This product currently exists as a test model.

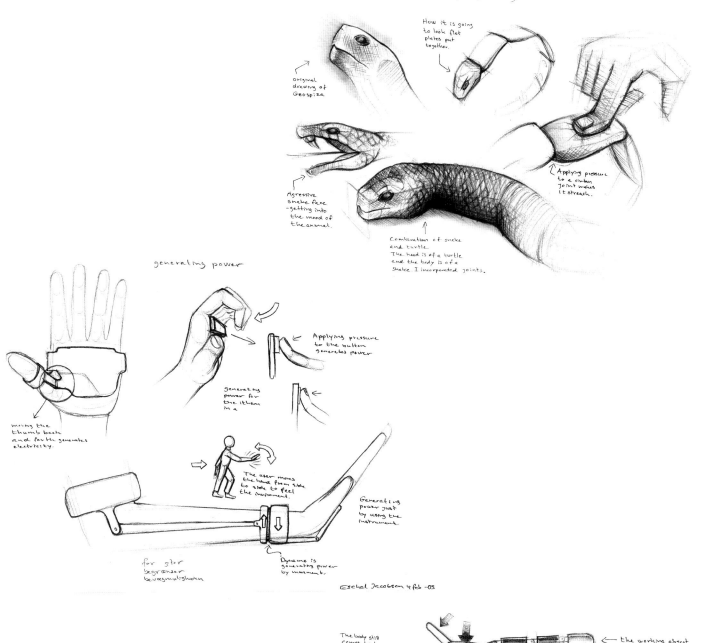

The designer modeled the 3YE on the snake, who, in some species, gathers visual information by means of infared receivers situated between the nostrils and the eye.

Ambient Experience

Stefano Marzano, Design Team (2005)
www.design.philips.com
info.design@philips.com

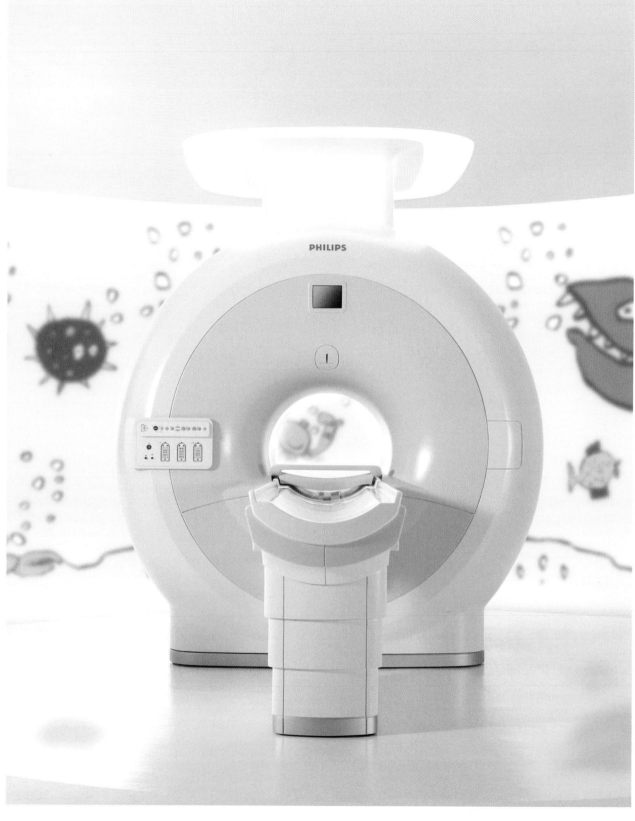

Going for a brain scan can be a stressful experience. The magnetic resonance imaging (MRI) equipment is imposing, and patients are alone in the examination room. The Ambient Experience for Healthcare is a complete multimedia environment that adapts to patients. When patients enter the MRI, the environment changes to match their personal needs through specific settings. Music and images are displayed, and adjustments to the whole lighting and ambience are made.

projected image. of sky
sky becomes a way
to communicate
with patient.

coil
selection.

transforming clouds.

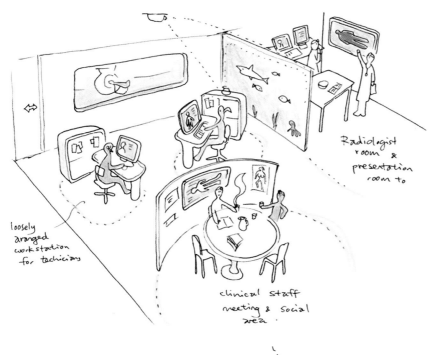

loosely
aranged
workstation
for technicians

clinical staff
meeting & social
area.

Radiologist
room &
presentation
room to

Staff
area

Super silent
MRI machine.

Tablet to perform
scan.

Top: The numbers in bubbles denote the countdown to the start of the scanning. Bottom: The preliminary sketches of the MRI included not only the scanner but also the layout of the items around it and how they interact with it.

Consistency of Shadows

Kevin Henry (IDSA), Anne Dorothee Boehme (2007)

khenry@colum.edu

The goal of this project was to push the boundaries of the catalog merging traditional print media with the richness of digital media, all on a tight budget, as well to create an object that would be unique yet still functional. The concept went through a brainstorming followed by physical mock-ups and refinement sketches and renderings. Several models and prototypes were also created. The catalog can be found in several museum collections.

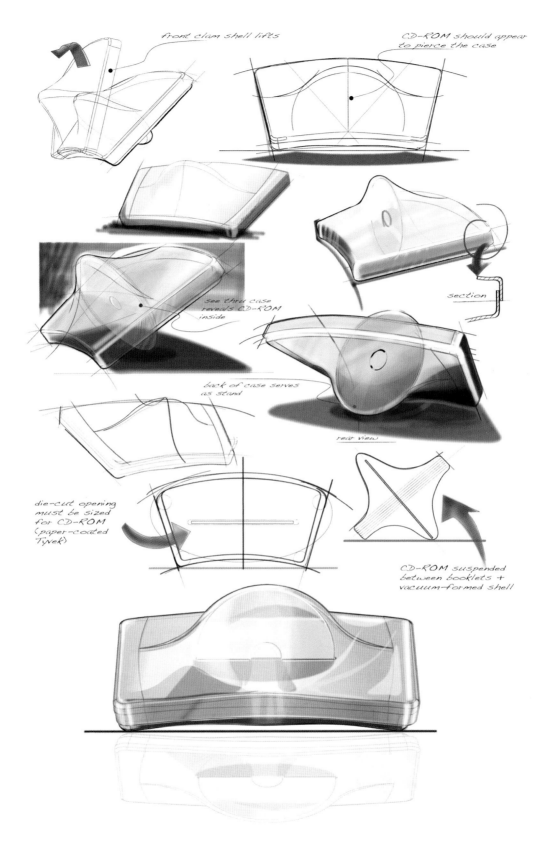

front clam shell lifts

CD-ROM should appear to pierce the case

see thru case reveals CD-ROM inside

section

back of case serves as stand

rear view

die-cut opening must be sized for CD-ROM (paper-coated Tyvek)

CD-ROM suspended between booklets + vacuum-formed shell

Sketches for the design of the catalog Consistency of Shadows, which explore the different ways of integrating the CD into a traditionally flat object.

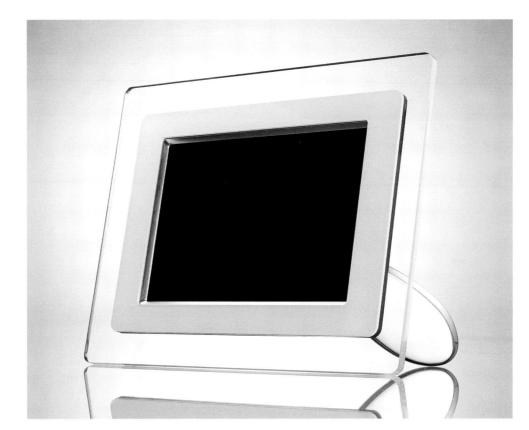

The Philips digital frame has a high-colored resolution screen that enables the user to share and visualize the photographs at all times and in all locations. It also includes interchangeable frames so that the user may integrate the product in the decoration of their home. There is the possibility of adjusting the angle of vision and hanging it on the wall or any other vertical surface. The user interface has been improved so that its use is much more intuitive.

Ergonomic Violin

Tricia Ho (2006)
tyche83t@hotmail.com

The Ergonomic Violin is a high-range electric violin made using carbon fiber. It can be customized with different exchangeable frames, making it adaptable to any user's needs. Manufactured with polymer that adapts to the shape of the user's neck, the violin also comes equipped with a self-supporting piece that lets users play the instrument without resting it beneath the chin at all. The support piece can be modified and accommodated as many times as desired.

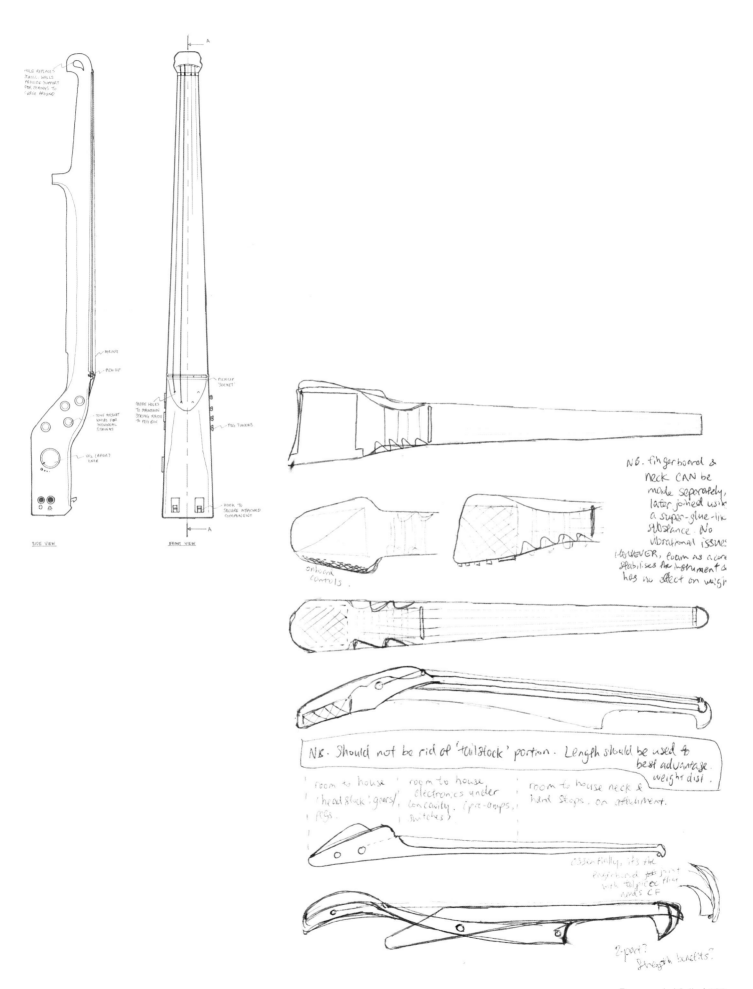

HOLE REPLACES SCROLL. WALLS PROVIDE SUPPORT FOR STRINGS TO CURVE AROUND

PERINTE

PICK-UP

SOME PRESENT NOBS FOR INDIVIDUAL STRINGS

VOL (BASIC) KNOB

SIDE VIEW

A

PICKUP 'SOCKET'

GUIDE HOLES TO MAINTAIN STRING KNOTS TO PEG BOX

PEG TUNERS

HOOK TO SECURE ATTACHED COMPONENT

A

FRONT VIEW

NB. fingerboard & neck CAN be made separately, later joined with a super-glue-like substance. No vibrational issues

HOWEVER, foam as a core stabilises the instrument & has no effect on weight

onboard controls.

NB. Should not be rid of 'tailstock' portion. Length should be used to best advantage. weight dist.

room to house 'headstock' gears/ pegs.

room to house electronics under concavity. (pre-amps, switches)

room to house neck & hand stops. on attachment.

essentially, it's the fingerboard joint with tailpiece that needs CF

2-part? strength benefits?

IBM Remote Projector

Kevin Kraemer (2005)
www.coroflot.com/kevinkraemer
kraemer.kevin@gmail.com

From the moment Kevin Kraemer began to work on this project, he sought to take a step closer to the evolution of normal projectors. First, he devised a list with the normal problems associated with this type of device. The IBM doesn't need to be connected to a computer; it only needs to be plugged into an electrical socket. Its integrated PDA works as a remote control and allows the user to move about and give more dynamic presentations. Because of its spherical design, it's simple to adjust the screen.

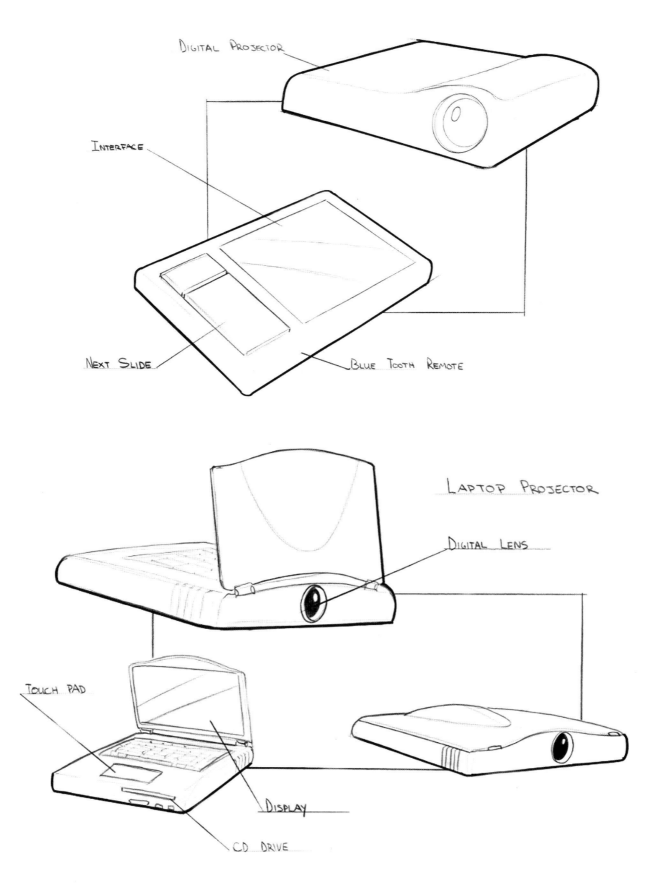

DIGITAL PROJECTOR

INTERFACE

NEXT SLIDE

BLUE TOOTH REMOTE

LAPTOP PROJECTOR

DIGITAL LENS

TOUCH PAD

DISPLAY

CD DRIVE

Jawbone

Fuseproject (2008)

www.fuseproject.com
info@fuseproject.com

Because of its noise suppression technology, the Jawbone earphones can be used in the noisiest environments. Comfortable and lightweight, the Jawbone has a stylish design that transforms it from a technological device and into a fashion accessory. Directed at a market sector interested in new technology, but also in avant-garde design, Jawbone has set the benchmark in the high technology accessory sector. Jawbone was awarded in 2008 with the Gold Award of the Sparks Awards, and was also mentioned as the Best Bluetooth Headset by the UK National TV the same year.

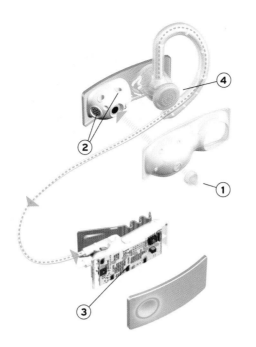

Two streamlined buttons control all the functions of the headset and are discretely hidden underneath the outside shield. The shield itself is textured in a sound reflective relief.

4-Stage Jawbone Technology Process

1. Sensor feels vibrations produced on cheek when speaking

2. Two microphones capture background sounds

3. Electronics & software (Jawbone clip) subtract unwanted noise so you can be heard

4. Jawbone enhances incoming speech, allowing it to stand out clearly above the noise of your background

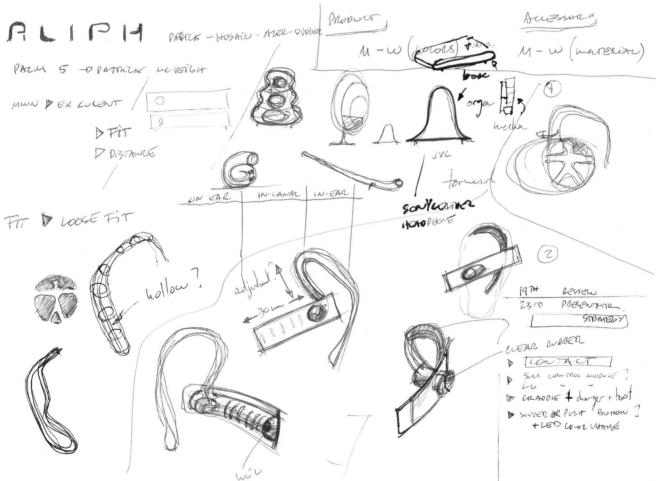

Previous sketches. The objective was to design a industry changing product and extend the innovative nature of the headset into the development of packaging and brand to cement a total brand experience.

Ladybug iPod Speaker Dock

Myk Lum, Yoon Kim/LDA (2007)

www.ldallc.com
mykl@ldallc.com

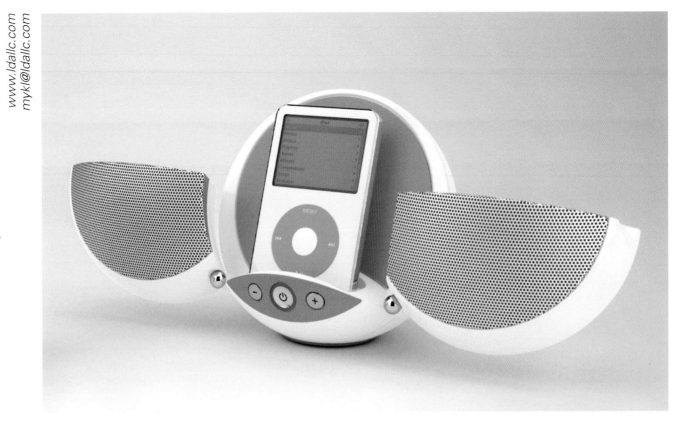

Specifically designed for the adolescent market, the Ladybug iPod Speaker Dock is a loudspeaker station for the iPod. Varnished with a layer of metallic paint, the foldaway wings of the loudspeakers give the product its own personality and make it a visual standout in a saturated market.

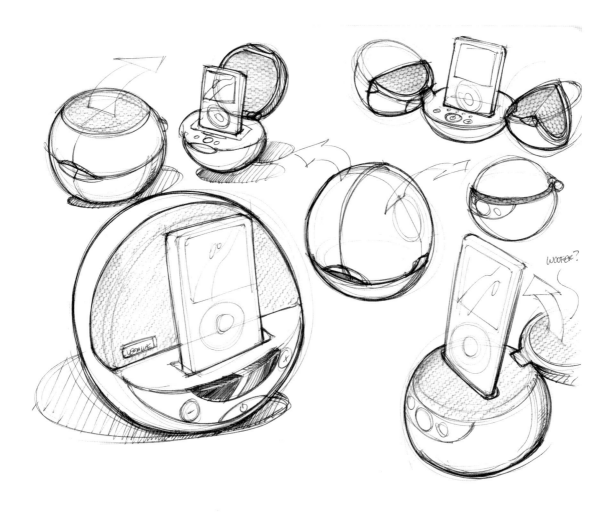

Speaker collapses into sphere shape when not in use

Close position

Open position

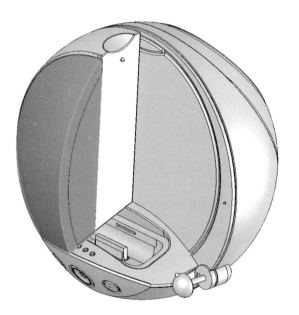

The "wings" of the loudspeakers fold out not only to give the product the sensation of movement but also to achieve higher quality stereo sound.

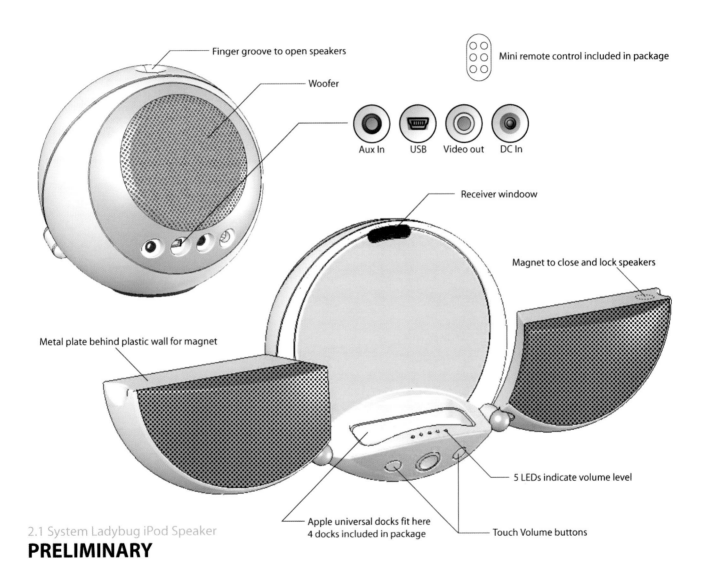

Finger groove to open speakers

Woofer

Mini remote control included in package

Aux In USB Video out DC In

Receiver windoow

Magnet to close and lock speakers

Metal plate behind plastic wall for magnet

5 LEDs indicate volume level

Apple universal docks fit here
4 docks included in package

Touch Volume buttons

2.1 System Ladybug iPod Speaker
PRELIMINARY

The Nargile water pipe is an update of a traditional product with a long history behind it. Because of its sleek, minimalist design, the pipe attracts a new audience than the market sector traditionally interested in this type of product. In fact, Nargile has been on display in several international expositions and shows, such as the Saint-Etienne International Design Biennale, and has been created with a more international, rather than local, market in mind.

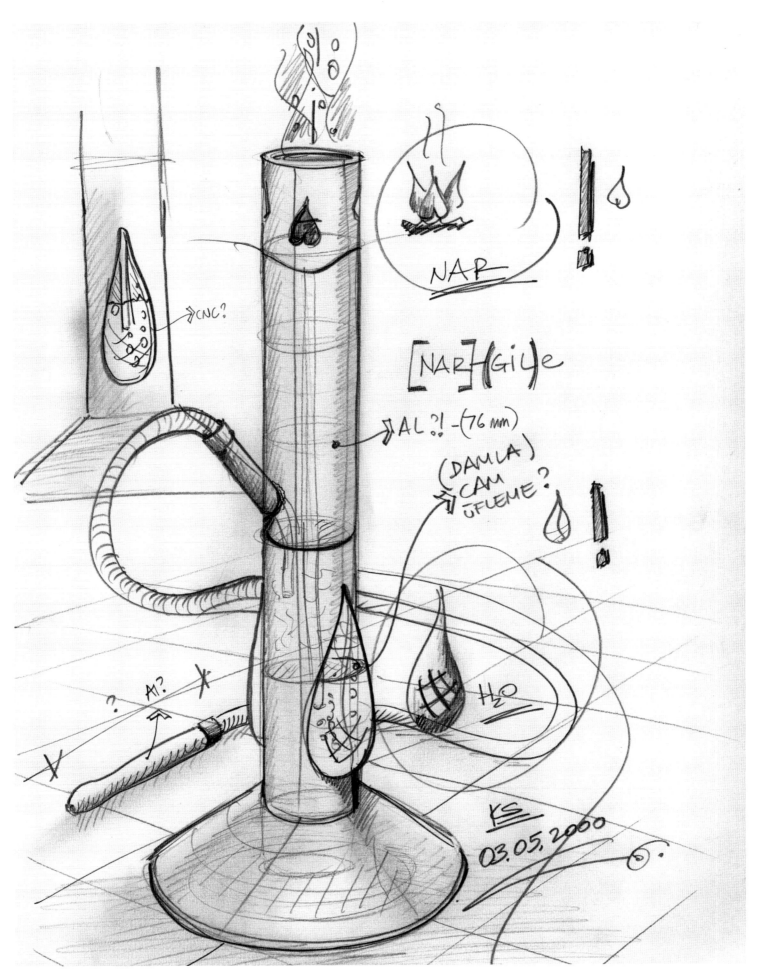

Netgear Platinum II

NewDealDesign, Gadi Amit (2006)
www.newdealdesign.com
info@newdealdesign.com

The Netgear Platinum II family of cases has been designed to store the majority of the peripherals produced by NewDealDesign. Its objectives are three-fold: lower manufacturing costs by 30 percent by reducing the amount of pieces from twenty-four to eight, improve the ventilation, and move forward in terms of peripheral designs. The base of the product allows it to be positioned vertically and hides the connections. The Netgear Platinum II is available in different sizes and colors.

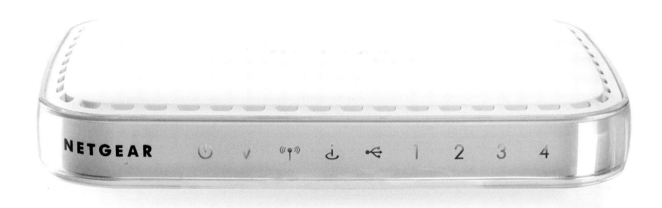

The mirror on the side of Netgear
Platinum II illuminates the pilot lights,
creating a halo of light. The effect
is both spectacular and innovating,
making the product worthy of many
international prizes.

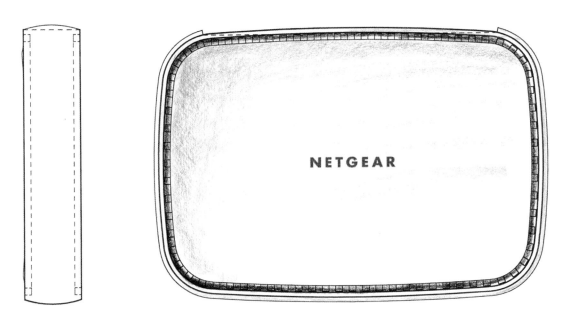

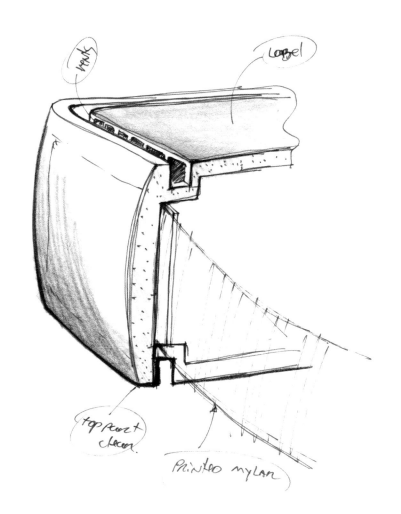

Plantronics Pulsar

One & Co (2006)
www.oneandco.com
hello@oneandco.com

Plantronics Pulsar are headphones that work by a voice and data transmission system between Bluetooth devices. Besides the fact that the headphones can be connected wirelessly, the user can switch between the mobile phone and the iPod by pushing a button. Designed for music lovers who want to be able to acess their mobile phone with the simple switch of a button, Plantronics Pulsar makes sure no one misses a beat.

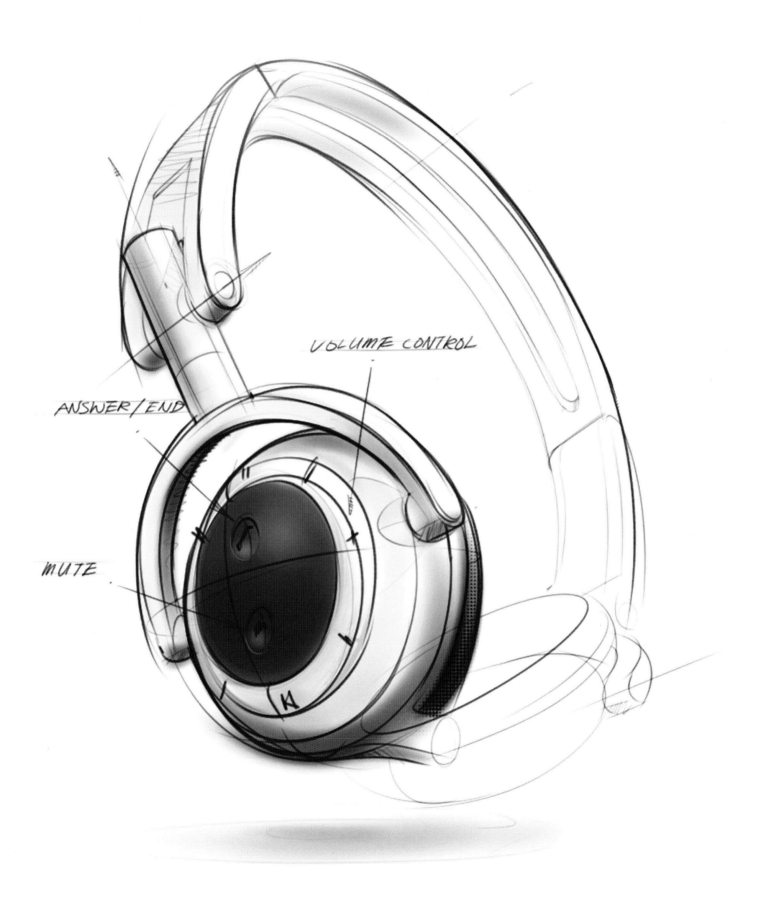

VOLUME CONTROL

ANSWER/END

MUTE

The first sketches and renderings of the headphones show how the location of the button enables the user to alternate between signals and the volume control.

Sabar

Michael Young (2007)
www.michael-young.com
contact@michael-young.com

Sabar is a black plastic vibrator with an ergonomic silhouette designed to provide the user with as much freedom of movement as possible. The vibrator is based on the concept of nodes and antinodes used in the physics of stationary waves (and that make reference to the point of the wave which has the minimum and maximum amplitude). Two fissures have been added to guarantee maximum possible vibration. The luminous light on the front of the gadget indicates the intensity and speed of the vibration.

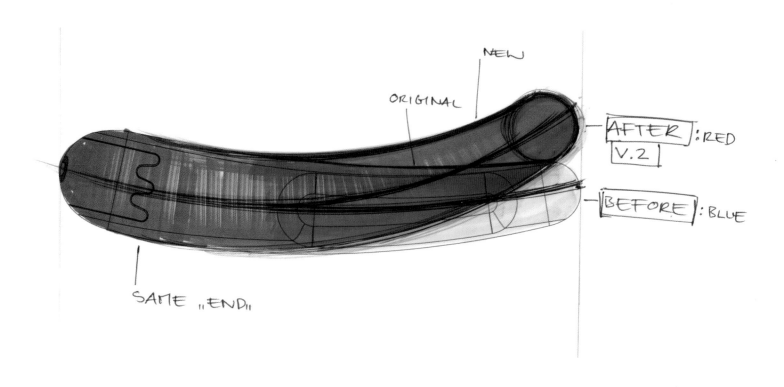

NEW

ORIGINAL

AFTER : RED

V.2

BEFORE : BLUE

SAME "END"

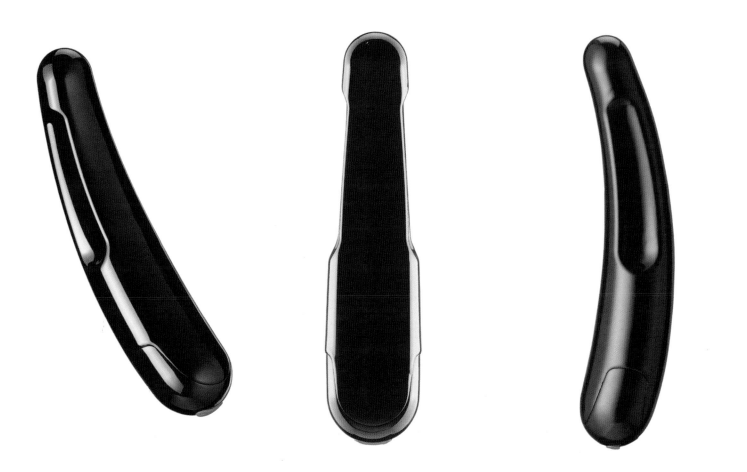

Scribble Scanner

Paul Sandip (2005)

www.coroflot.com/paulsandip, www.differentialdesign.blogspot.com
differentialdesign@yahoo.com

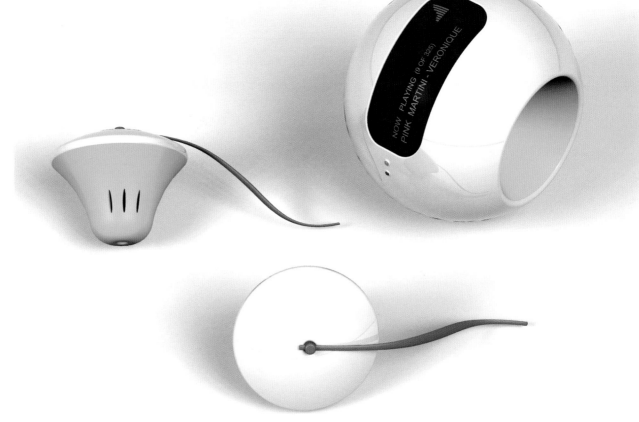

Designer Paul Sandip created the Scribble Scanner based on the idea that technology must be dreamt about before being designed. The Scribble Scanner, in this sense, performs above and beyond the casual scanner. This multifunctional device can be either a pencil or a pen, and it scans and registers everything that the user writes so that it can be later uploaded digitally. In addition to its Bluetooth technology, it can store data and transfer it in the same way as a mobile phone. Scribble Scanner is also an alarm clock, an MP3 player, and a voice recorder.

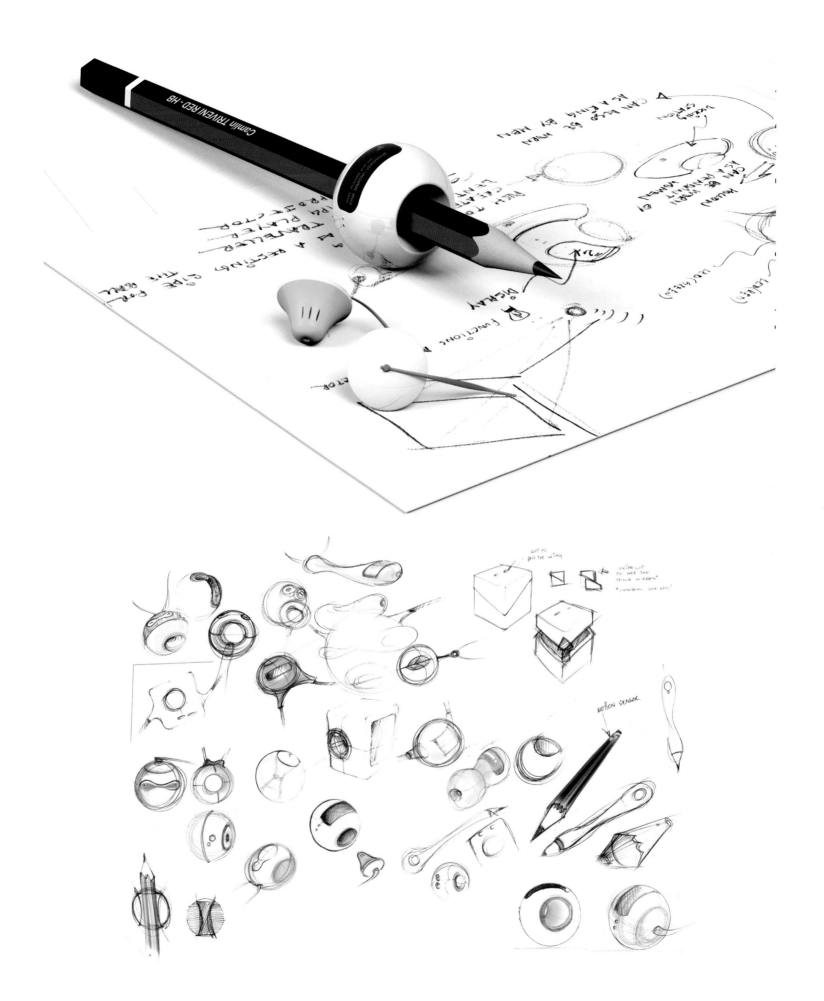

Camlin TRUVEN RED - HB

SimpleDrive

Stuart Karten Design (2008)
www.kartendesign.com
info@kartendesign.com

SimpleDrive represents one step further toward environmental sustainability. Based on the idea of "simplicity," this hard drive and its various components have been slimmed down. The peripheral is small; the components are few. Its curved outline assists the production process, the grooves on the back offer ventilation and improve its efficiency, and, most importantly, it can be recycled once its life is over.

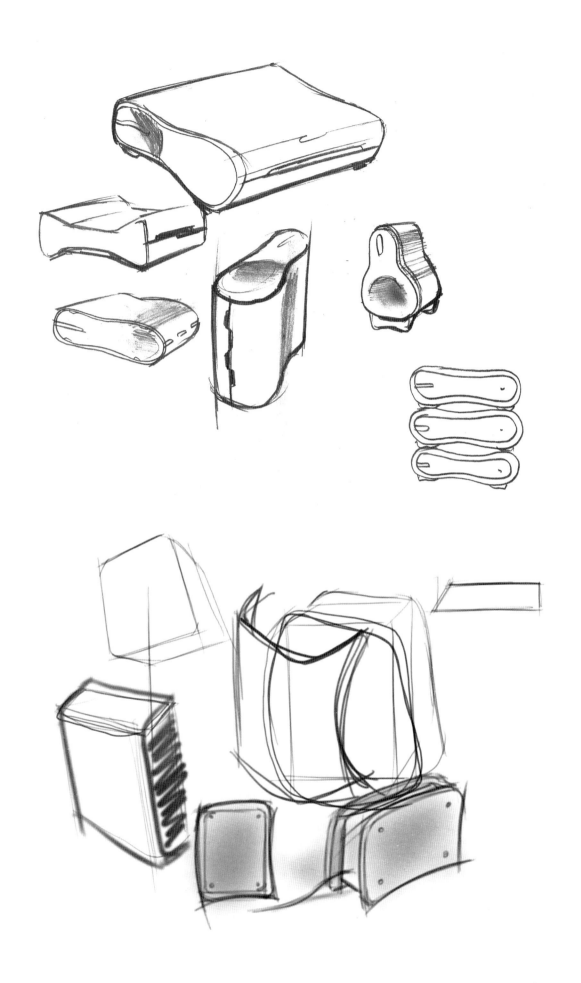

SteriShoe ™

Brook Middlecott Banham (2008)
www.middlecott.com, www.brookbanham.com
brook@middlecott.com

SteriShoe™ is a device that removes odor from shoes by a system of ultraviolet germicidal irradiation (UVC). The objective is to avoid using chemical products. The device also doubles up as a conventional shoehorn that prevents shoes from going out of shape over time. The initial sketches were carried out by Brook Middlecott Banham together with the product's industrial design team.

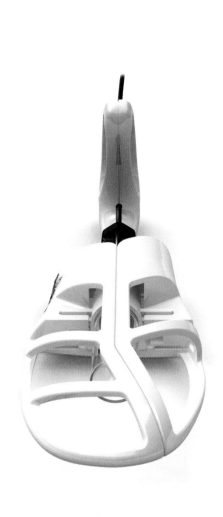

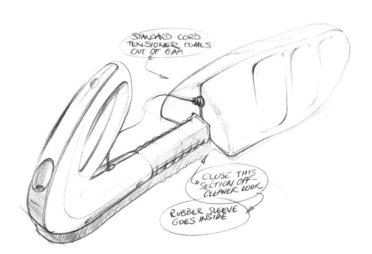

STANDARD CORD
TENSIONER COMES
OUT OF GAP.

CLOSE THIS
SECTION OFF-
CLEANER LOOK

RUBBER SLEEVE
GOES INSIDE

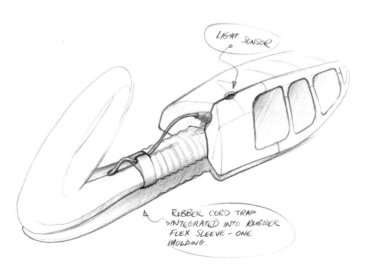

LIGHT SENSOR

RUBBER CORD TRAP
DINTEGRATED INTO RUBBER
FLEX SLEEVE - ONE
MOLDING.

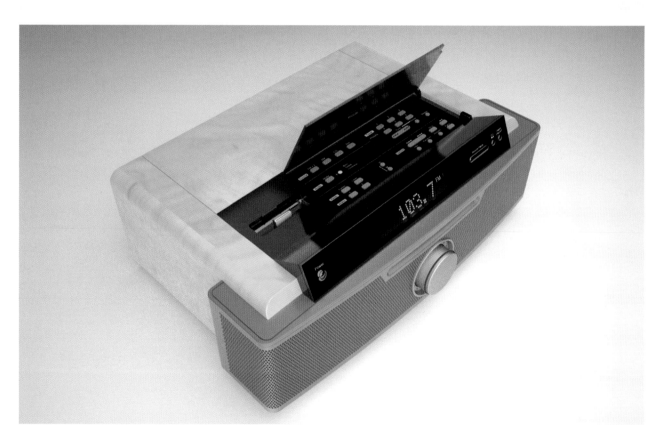

When analyzing the table radio market, designer Myk Lum discovered that many had been made using low-cost plastic. From that moment forward, Myk Lum wanted to create an upscale product, one that appeared to be more like a piece of furniture than an electronic device, a radio that would be valued for both its function and its design. Easy-to-use, Table Radio hides the non-essential controls under a panel.

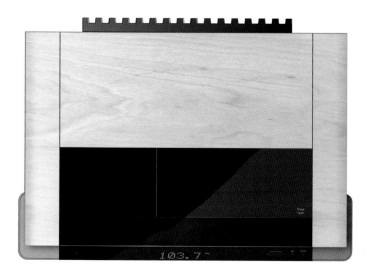

ANGLED
CUT

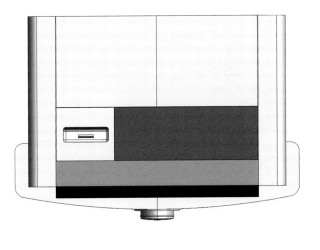

To study the location and the
positioning of the internal elements
of the radio, a 3-D-CAD model created,
seen here.

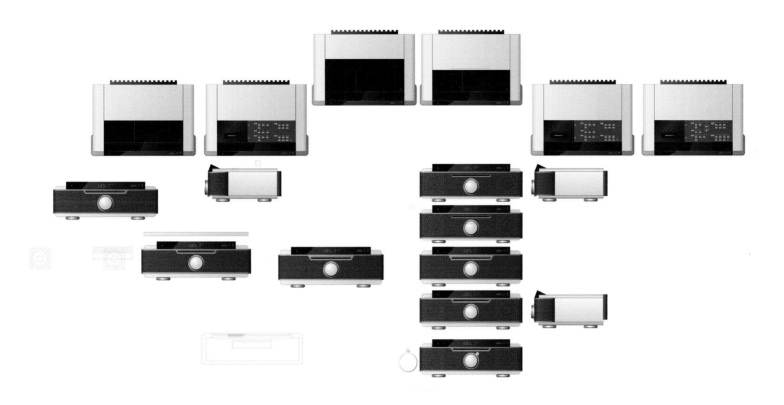

Talktool

Jedco (2005)
www.jedco.co.uk
info@jedco.co.uk

With the objective of launching an attractive, cordless designer telephone, capable of being used in any car, in the office, or at home, Jedco carried out dozens of sketches preceded by a wide and comprehensive market study. Later, these sketches were developed and perfected together with a team of engineers until they came up with an "easy-to-use" concept. The result? Talktool. Simple. Compact. And cutting-edge.

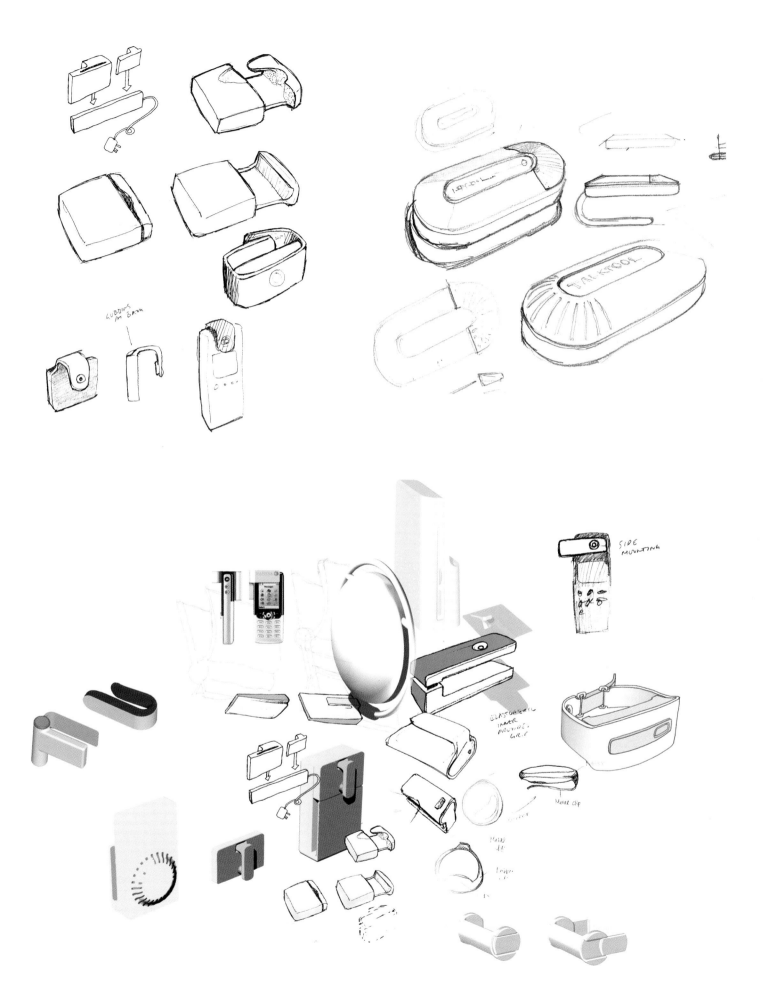

Touch Diamond

One & Co, HTC (2008)

www.oneandco.com
hello@oneandco.com

Touch Diamond is the latest generation of mobile phone that has placed its manufacturer, HTC, as a global leader in the demanding market of the Internet mobile. The modern design of Touch Diamond disregards all unnecessary accessories, allowing the user to focus on its innovative interface. The outer cover of the phone resembles the look and feel of a diamond, elevating the device from a techie gadget to a fashion must-have.

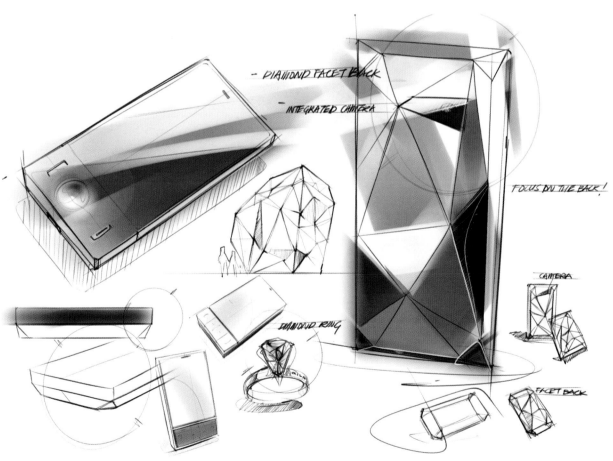

XFX XGear Controller

Stuart Karten Design (2005)

www.kartendesign.com
info@kartendesign.com

With a design that departs from the toy-like aesthetic of competitors, the XFX XGear Controller was tailored for mature gamers. Stuart Karten Design used sport rubber grips, refined metallic finishes, and illuminated buttons to create a sophisticated aesthetic.

The controller's rounded shape allows players a high level of mobility around the play pad. The centrally placed battery rests on the player's hand for balance and comfort. Control keys are positioned for ready access in repeat functions.

To reach the final design of the XFX
XGear Controller (third and fourth
drawing from the top), several models
were studied and sketched before
eventually being rejected.

Zon Hearing Aid

Stuart Karten Design (2008)

www.kartendesign.com
info@kartendesign.com

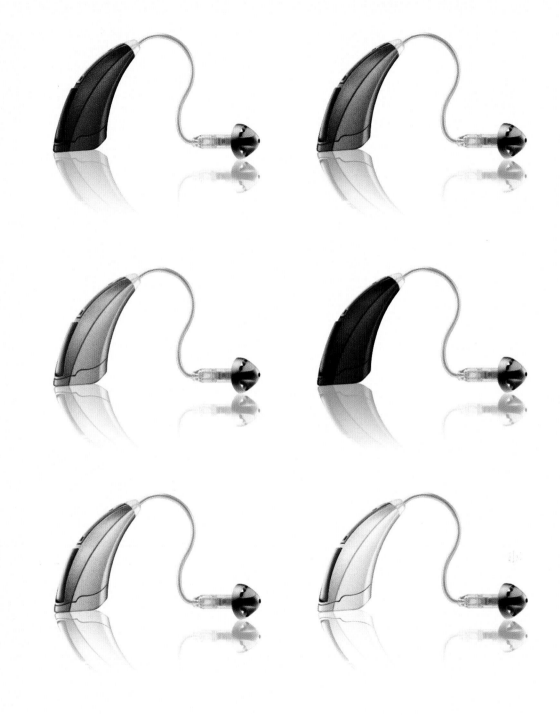

Stuart Karten Design has changed the perception of the hearing aid with this modern and stylish design. With her innovative design, hearing aids have gone from being objects that help beat the stigma associated with hearing disabilities. Zon Hearing Aid has been designed as a piece of jewelry and is bathed in shiny, metallic paint. With six different color tones to blend in as much as possible with the user's hair color, its sinuous shape is totally ergonomic and the device is virtually invisible once placed behind the ear.

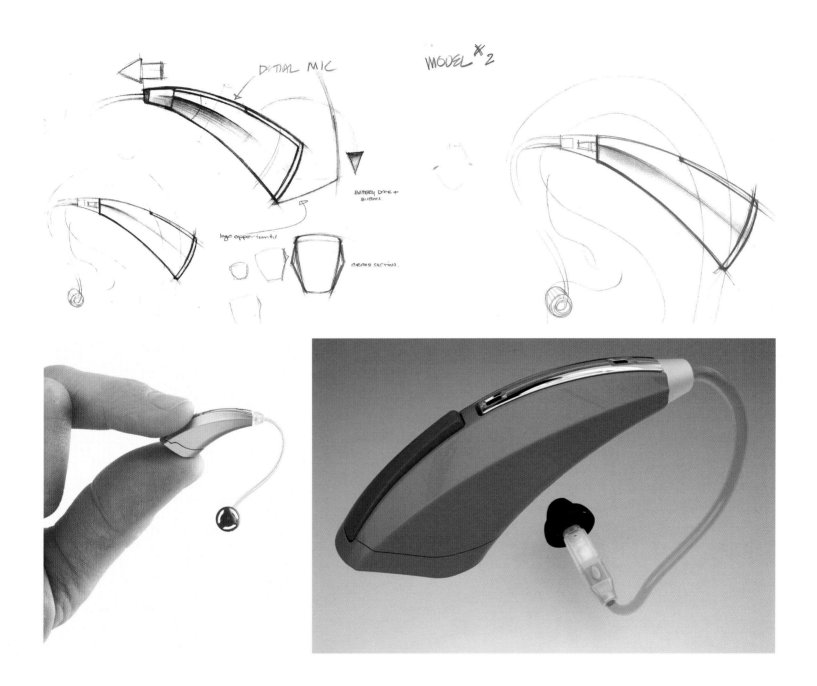

Urban
Architecture
and Design

Baumhaus World of Living

Andreas Wenning/Baumraum (2008)

www.baumraum.de
a.wenning@baumraum.de

The treehouse's static system is based on two elements: the elliptically shaped treehouse rests not in the oak itself, but on seven angled and conically shaped supports made of Siberian larch. The supports are hinged to the treehouse and concrete foundation and stand at different angles to each other. Unlike the treehouse itself, the loads of the terrace and stairs are braced by the tree. From the terrace, a catwalk leads to the higher treehouse.

The vaulted interior is wallpapered with a photo mural of the surrounding oak tree, to give the illusion of the outdoors indoors. There are blocks of inspirational text written on the walls in German, English, and French.

During the design phase, a vast number of framework variants were simulated using models and then finessed with the help of a complex computer system.

Johnston C200

Phil Cook (2006)
www.formfoundry.co.uk
phil@formfoundry.co.uk

Johnston Sweepers asked Form Foundry to redesign their compact cleaning vehicle. The project was carried out from the sketches and 3-D CAD designs by Phil Cook, together with hyper-realistic photographic montages. From an aesthetic point of view, the interior panels were designed so that a minimum number of molds were required. Externally, the objective was to give the vehicle a more contemporary and defined shape than the previous model, which was more diluted and impersonal.

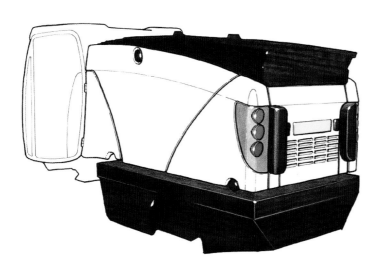

Drawings and sketches of the cabin and digital renders of the Johnston C200. The final design was not too dissimilar to the first digital representations of the vehicle.

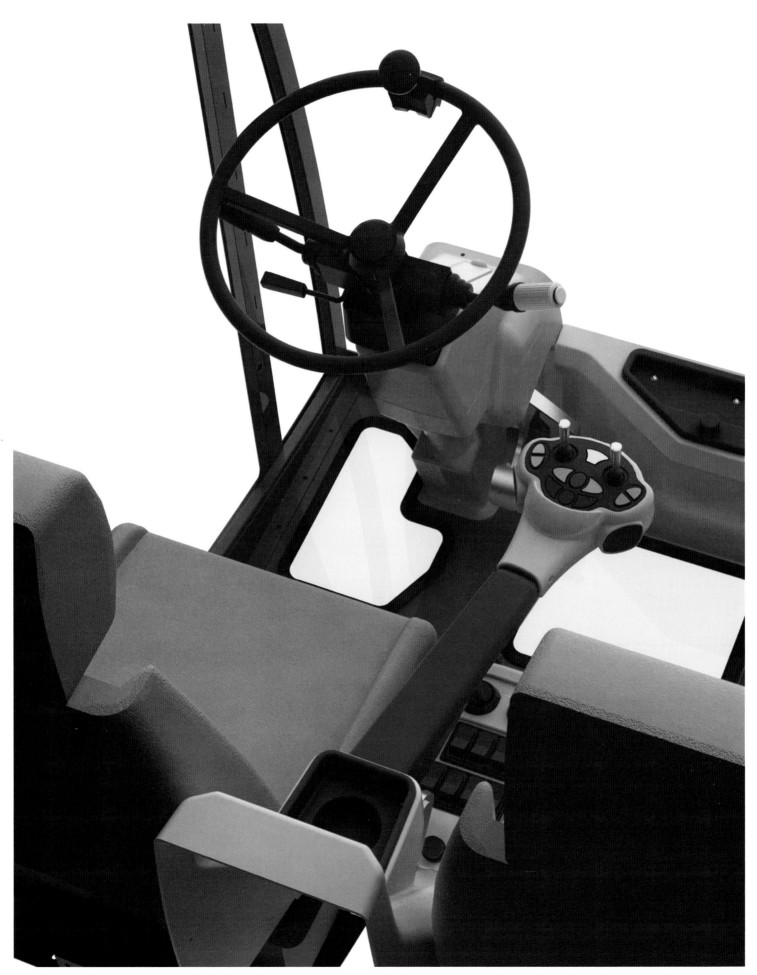

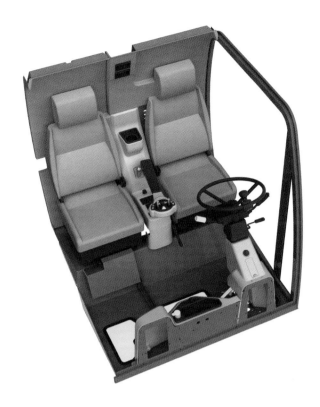

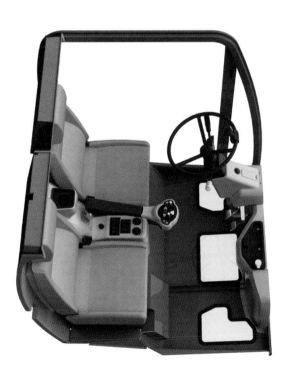

Reducing the amount of molds and pieces that the vehicle is made from not only helps lower costs, but also standardizes the overall design.

Life 01USG is a prefabricated, economic modular home designed for two to three people. The modules are flexible and can be extended by adding other modules, in addition to being ecologically sustainable. The home has three levels: the entrance and a small garden area are on the first level; public or shared areas, such as the kitchen and reading rooms, are on the second level; bathrooms and living rooms are on the third level; and the upper level houses the private area with two bedrooms, a study, and cupboard.

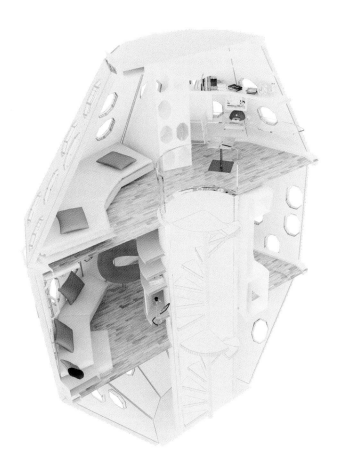

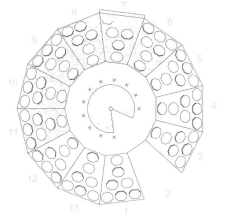

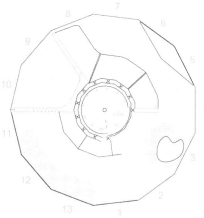

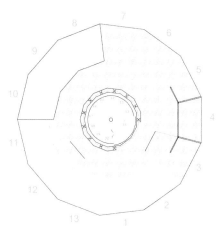

Drawings and 3-D cross-section
renderings. Not only is Life 01USG
a real house, it is also a study on low-
cost building alternatives for houses
that need to be built quickly.

Life 01USG is a cheap, ecological option that can be built relatively quickly, ideal for overpopulated urban environments.

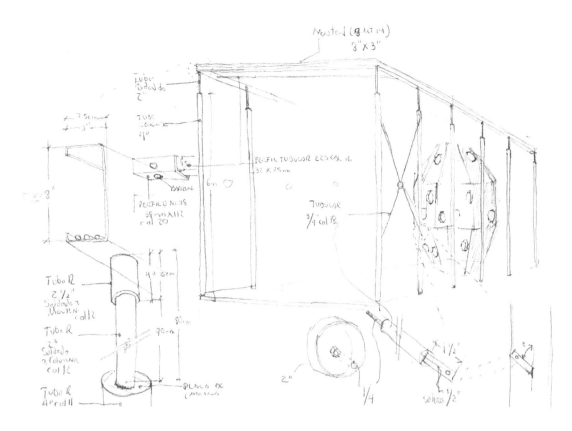

Sketch and 3-D digital image which show the possibility of the Life 01USG units being anchored to conventional buildings using simple attachment systems.

New Bus Shelter for London

Jedco (2008)
www.jedco.co.uk
info@jedco.co.uk

When the coordinating London public transport company launched a contest for the design of a new bus stop, Jedco decided to enter. The shelter had to meet a series of requirements: it had to be secure, informative, and flexible. Jedco incorporated solar panels, ticket dispensers, and an independent lighting system into its design. The selected building materials were chosen because they were durable, making them less susceptible to being destroyed by the elements and vandalism. Many of Jedco's innovative features have been incorporated into the city's bus stops.

ENCOURAGE
WALKING.

PRIORITY SEATING.

WHERE?
HOW TO SHOW

PERCH

SEAT.

WHEEL CHAIR PARKING SPACE

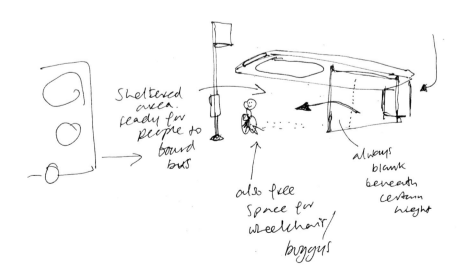

Sheltered
area.
ready for
people to
board
bus

also free
space for
wheelchair/
buggys

always
blank
beneath
certain
height

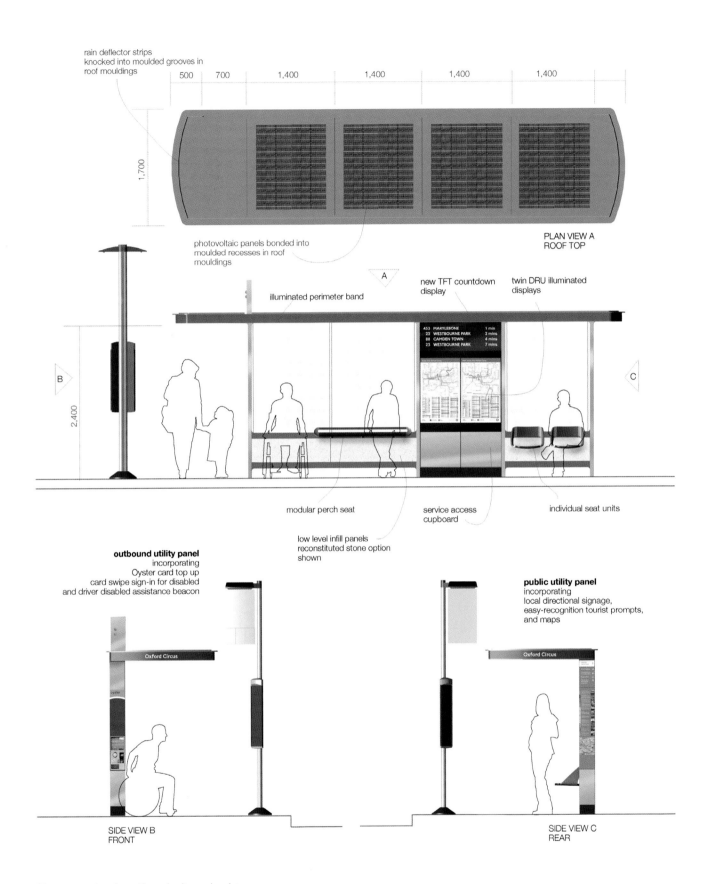

rain deflector strips
knocked into moulded grooves in
roof mouldings

500   700   1,400   1,400   1,400   1,400

1,700

photovoltaic panels bonded into
moulded recesses in roof
mouldings

PLAN VIEW A
ROOF TOP

A

illuminated perimeter band

new TFT countdown
display

twin DRU illuminated
displays

453   MARYLEBONE   1 min
23   WESTBOURNE PARK   2 mins
88   CAMDEN TOWN   4 mins
23   WESTBOURNE PARK   7 mins

B

2,400

C

modular perch seat

service access
cupboard

individual seat units

low level infill panels
reconstituted stone option
shown

outbound utility panel
incorporating
Oyster card top up
card swipe sign-in for disabled
and driver disabled assistance beacon

public utility panel
incorporating
local directional signage,
easy-recognition tourist prompts,
and maps

Oxford Circus

Oxford Circus

SIDE VIEW B
FRONT

SIDE VIEW C
REAR

By contest rules, the shelters had to
be flexible enough to be adaptable to
urban environments and be accessible
to all types of users.

Typical 2 Bay BTK Shelter

1 Mono-crystaline photovoltaic panel, 180 Wp. Flush fitting to roof for ease of cleaning.

2 Modular roof carcase. recycled structural HDPE moulding, with facility for glass panel, and rain deflector strips.

3 Translucent illuminated red perimeter band panels.

4 Internal ceiling panel, acts as reflector for ambient lighting.

5 Encapsulated solid state LED strips, illuminate both roof ceiling and red perimeter band.

6 Roof underside perimeter panels, holds glazing, and covers roof duct carrying LED strips, discreet CCTV, RF antenna, cabling and hidden acoustic attenuator.

7 Fabricated stainless steel modular cantilevered frame.

8 Side interactive panels, options for carrying printed or internally illuminated local wayfinding panels, Help point or Oyster top up facilities.

9 6.0mm thick toughened glazing panels.

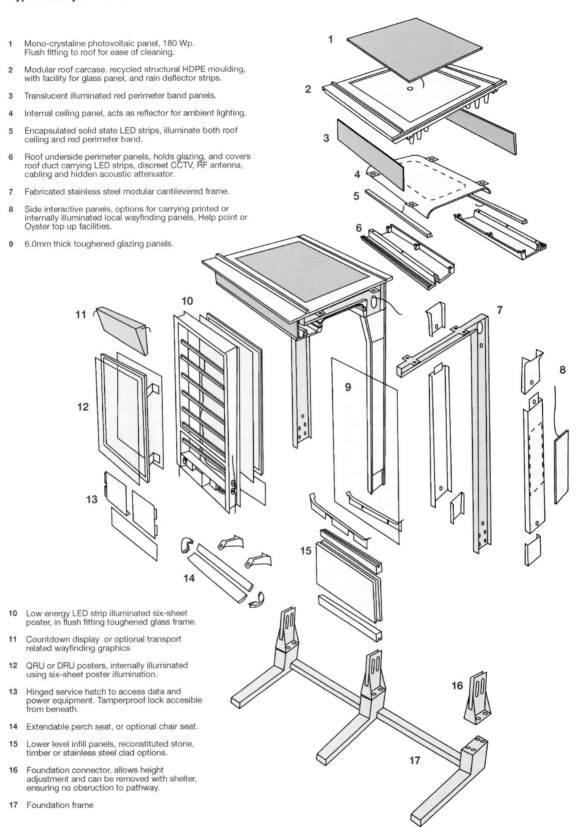

10 Low energy LED strip illuminated six-sheet poster, in flush fitting toughened glass frame.

11 Countdown display or optional transport related wayfinding graphics

12 QRU or DRU posters, internally illuminated using six-sheet poster illumination.

13 Hinged service hatch to access data and power equipment. Tamperproof lock accesible from beneath.

14 Extendable perch seat, or optional chair seat.

15 Lower level infill panels, reconstituted stone, timber or stainless steel clad options.

16 Foundation connector, allows height adjustment and can be removed with shelter, ensuring no obsruction to pathway.

17 Foundation frame

Children between the ages of seven to fourteen years demand challenge, stimulation, and differentiation. With these challenges in mind, Designworks Windsor has designed an exciting and innovative collection of senior playground equipment that channels and encourages the energy of older children. Nexus fuses organic forms and a striking, raw architectural styles to create structures that will stimulate action and excite any imagination. The sci-fi look instinctively appeals to children's sense of adventure.

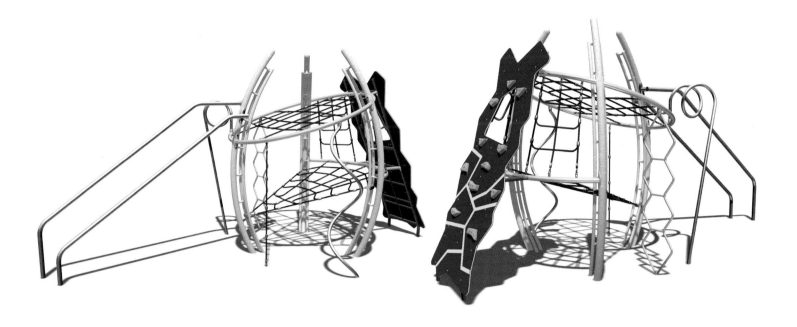

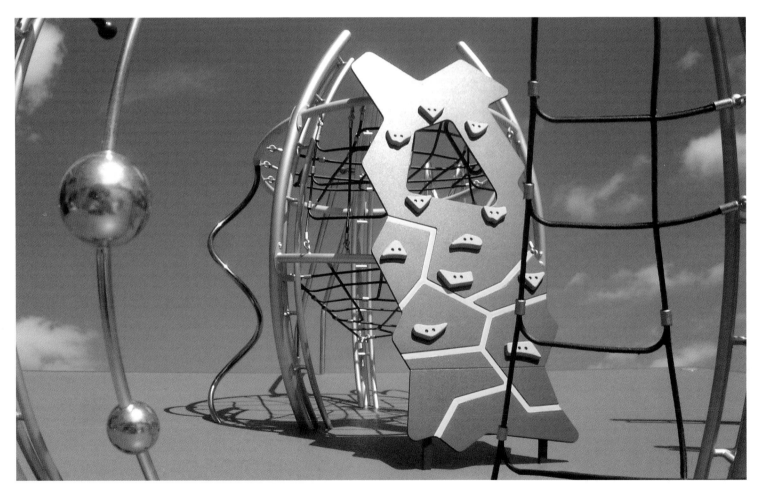

The preliminary sketches and renders help to facilitate the visualization of the relation between height, width, and length of the different elements that make up Nexus.

www.baumraum.de
a.wenning@baumraum.de

Andreas Wenning/Baumraum (2008)

Palm Fiction

Palm Fiction is a unit project for one or several palm trees. Made of a spherical structure, the Palm Fiction hangs approximately 16.4 feet off the ground from a palm tree by steel cables and resistant fabric straps.

The unit has a transparent and retractable cover, lateral points of light, a bed, a minibar, a terrace, and hi-fi equipment.

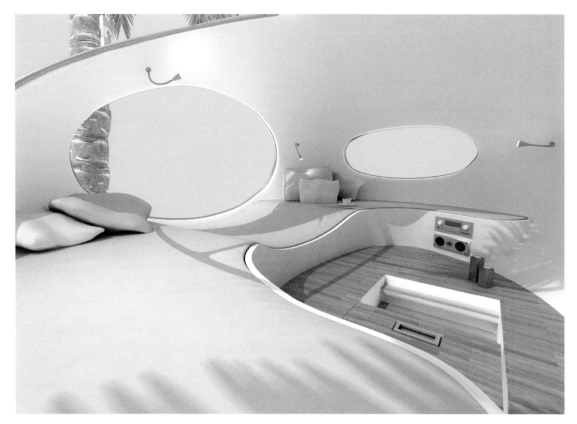

From the terrace, a second stair leads to the bottom of the cabin through a hatch. The construction of glass fiber reinforced plastic and aluminium can be fixed to other trees by steel-cables and textile-belts.

Palm trees are capable of withstanding weights greater that the Palm Fiction; in order to give the structure more stability, however, its weight is distributed over three trees.

Pod Mk2

Phil Cook (2005)

www.formfoundry.co.uk
phil@formfoundry.co.uk

Pod Caravans is a British manufacturer of fiberglass and retro caravans inspired by designs from the thirties to the sixties. The Mk2 model was designed so that it would be easier to manufacture than previous models. Its modular construction enabled different panels to be added, such as the extendable roof. The design of the MK2, in particular, was inspired by the futuristic aesthetics of the "Space-Age" seventies look, and is the result of work based on the sketches designed by Phil Cook.

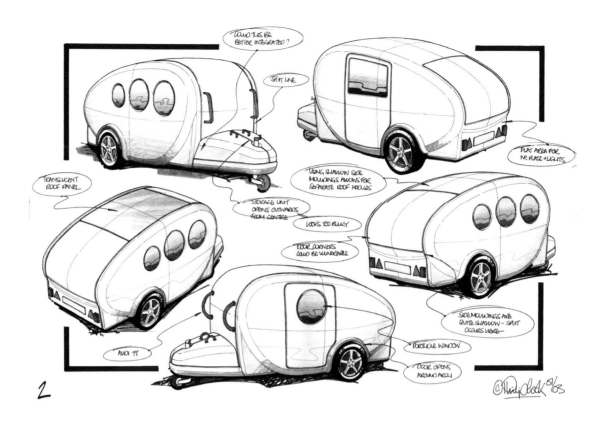

2

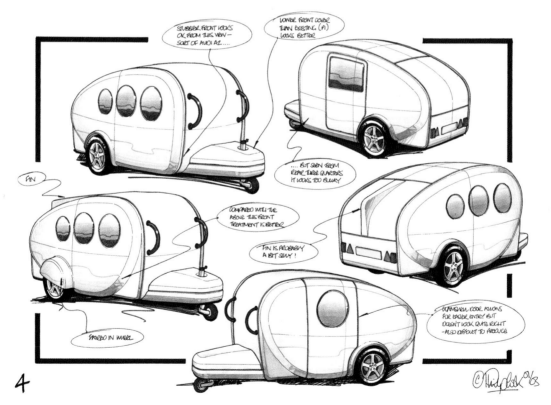

4

The Duck Family

Splitterwerk (2005)

www.splitterwerk.at
splitterwerk@splitterwerk.at

Duck is an individual two-levels house in the form of a duck. The first level is the living area, and the second, accessed by a staircase, is a small viewpoint or attic (duck eyes being windows of this attic). In the own words of Splitterwerk designers: "Multi-incident shells are switchable structures enhanced by events. The individual apartments can be added to, stacked on top of and linked with one another. The design of the outside space results from the requirement of the internal spaces."

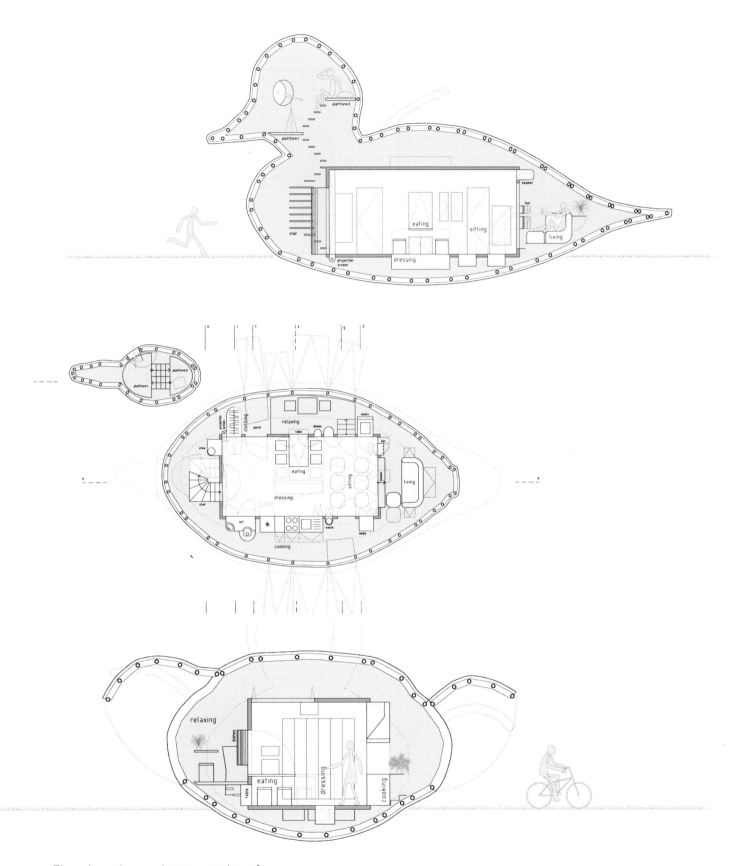

Elevation, plan, and cross section of a
conventional duck house. Designers
state: "The question of the proportions,
size, and rhythm of the facade has
become obsolete."

www.baumraum.de
a.wenning@baumraum.de

Winding Snake

Andreas Wenning/Baumraum (2008)

The Sequoia Sempervirens are giant trees that reach heights of over 328 feet. These trees are the setting for the design Winding Snake. The treehouse comprises a staircase, which winds like a snake around a sequoia trunk, ending in a closed, double-storey cabin.

At mid-height, there is an elliptically-shaped terrace. The weight of the entire construction is transferred to textile straps via steel cables. The dimensions of these trees allow them to bear far greater weights than this.

Sequoias can reach tremendous heights. The renders help to rapidly visualize how the spiral structure fixed to a tree of this size will adapt and what degree of inclination it will have to have.

The structure hangs from the tree by steel cables. The towering height of the giant sequoia enables these trees to support weights much greater than the Winding Ssnake.